a year at Brandywine Cottage

a year at Brandywine Cottage

SIX SEASONS *of* BEAUTY, BOUNTY, AND BLOOMS

David L. Culp

WITH Denise Cowie
PHOTOGRAPHS BY Rob Cardillo

Timber Press | Portland, Oregon

FOR GARDENERS, AND
EVERYONE WHO ENJOYS
CONNECTING WITH
NATURE TWELVE MONTHS
A YEAR

and

FOR VITA (FEBRUARY 2014–
JUNE 2019), WHO LOVED
THE GARDEN

Published in 2020 by Timber Press, Inc.
The Haseltine Building
133 S.W. Second Avenue, Suite 450
Portland, Oregon 97204-3527
timberpress.com

Printed in China
Text design by Hillary Caudle
Cover design by Mia Johnson and Hillary Caudle
Endpaper illustration by Kaitlin Pond

ISBN 978-1-60469-856-5

Catalog records for this book are available from the Library of
Congress and the British Library.

Contents

Prologue

IT SEEMS JUST A SHORT TIME AGO that I was standing outside an historic house, its paint peeling and everything about it calling for some serious TLC. I knew I could provide that. The cottage spoke to me at once. Its simple lines were so refined, and to me it offered many possibilities. We were in love ... and 30 years have passed.

Occasionally, people have asked me *What have you done with your life?* I made a garden. Along the way, I've met some wonderful people—and I can prove that because you are reading this book. I count myself most fortunate to have made a career out of doing something that I love. I made a garden, trying to make a difference in the process, and it changed me. As the many years pass, I seem to be melding into it, and I believe that is the best we can ask—to be at one with where we are.

I have had many successes, but I have had disappointments as well. I've lost numerous plants. I've had ideas that didn't work out right away. But the dreaming and the process outweighed all the disappointments. The process has been the most fun of all—observing countless facets of nature, from the dew glistening on a spider's web at sunrise to a firefly display at dusk.

It has not been a static 30 years; we don't work in a static art form. Plants are a living medium. They grow, they bloom, they die, and that gives each season a different dimension. The changing of the seasons gives us so many more reasons to enjoy the garden. If the seasons were all the same, we would have nothing to look forward to, and perhaps no sense of urgency to enjoy them as much.

So why have I chosen to break this book into six seasons? Science tells us that our Earth has four seasons, thanks to the planet's axial tilt: as it orbits the sun, the Earth tilts at a 23.5-degree angle to its orbital plane. Without that tilt, we wouldn't experience the changes we call seasons, and life on earth may have developed much differently. Four days each year mark the transition from one season to the next: in the northern hemisphere, the solstices in June and December mark the longest and shortest days, and the equinoxes in March and September represent the midway points between them. (In the southern hemisphere, of course, the seasons are reversed.)

However, knowing that the calendar says yesterday was winter and today is spring doesn't mean much to gardeners—or their gardens. The northern hemisphere garden in mid-March likely looks much more like the garden in April than it looks like the garden of January, yet January and most of March share the same wintry season. Seasonal transitions are much more subtle than the calendar implies and may be different not only from region to region, but from garden to garden. Even from one area of the garden to another. Don't we often rely on microclimates within our gardens to grow prized plants that might not otherwise survive in our zone? Plants respond as they always have—not to human constraints but to moisture, to temperature, to the amount of sun, to the length of daylight.

One directive that I repeat often throughout this book is *Look closer!* God is in the detail, according to the old saying, and the same may be said of our gardens: full enjoyment comes from looking at everything more closely, from seeking out the details that enrich the big picture. Looking closely has allowed me to know my garden intimately, from admiring something in bloom almost every day of the year to knowing what plants will thrive in the allelopathic soil under my pair of black walnut trees. And the more I observe my garden, the more it seems that four seasons are not enough. That division seems superimposed in an arbitrary way. The garden, after all, is a two-way conversation. We must listen and react as well as create. By looking closely at my garden over a period of time, and allowing it to speak to me, I find that the garden at Brandywine Cottage wants six seasons. As you will see, this book chronicles what happens in my garden over the course of those seasons.

I am not the first person to presume to change the calendar or to interpret the garden through the lives of plants. I refer you particularly to German nurseryman Karl Foerster (1874–1970), who saw his garden as having six seasons, although his observed dates that differ from mine. Foerster, one of my gardening heroes, was dedicated to gardening, and he helped transform his hometown of Bornim (now part of Potsdam) into a gardening mecca. His ideas on naturalistic garden design, revolutionary for their time, had an impact on other German cities, and ultimately on gardens in America. Wolfgang Oehme and James van Sweden, who popularized the New American Garden style, were partially influenced by Foerster's love of naturalistic plantings of grasses and perennials. Not a great deal has been written about Foerster in English, but according to published reports, he employed Jewish friends at his nursery during World War II and certainly resisted the Nazis' dictum to grow and sell primarily "pure" German plants. Foerster took a global view: he used plants from all over the world in his designs. Fittingly, the perennial grass named after him, *Calamagrostis* ×*acutiflora* 'Karl Foerster', is now found in gardens around the world.

But even Foerster wasn't the first to rearrange the seasons. In some tropical regions, only two seasons are traditionally recognized, "wet" and "dry." The ancient Egyptians observed three seasons based on their agricultural cycle—summer, winter, and inundation, timed to when the Nile flooded each year. Ancient Greeks used various calendars, mostly linked to lunar cycles and solar events, but agriculture relied on a seasonal calendar, which cataloged recurring weather changes that coincided with the movement of the stars. Other civilizations based their seasons on what we know as phenology, the study of cyclical natural phenomena, such as when plants bloom or birds migrate. Even now, many of our seasonal celebrations, such as cherry blossom festivals, rely on such empirical data.

Recent studies show that, for a variety of complex reasons including climate change, the seasons are shifting. The swings between summer and winter temperatures are wider in recent decades, spring seems to begin as much as a week earlier, and as much as I observe, I'm aware that times are changing in my own garden. In my classes at Longwood Gardens, one of the most frequently asked questions runs like this: "What weeks do these plants bloom?" My response is that I can give only an approximation, because bloom time is going to vary from year to year based on climactic and cultural conditions. The best I can do is a calculated guess. You cannot do bloom sequencing by the calendar; you do it by the garden. Plants have their own timetables. I cannot plan an iris festival for a specific week in June, as the iris may not cooperate. Or consider snowdrops: their bloom time may be off by two weeks, depending on the winter. I can only tell you what is most likely.

How many seasons does your garden have? No matter where you live, from the Northeast to the Southwest, I invite you to read your garden—let it speak to you. Perhaps it will show you it has four seasons, or maybe just three, or even six. But listen to what it tells you. Many things fall outside our human interpretation of time, and this may become even more apparent as we live with the challenges of climate

change. The most important thing is to look closely, at your garden and at the natural world around you. You are a participant in your garden, and by extension in the global garden that we all share. This is something all gardeners need to think about as climate change becomes more of a reality. We contributed to the problem. We must be accountable for our actions and become part of the solution. For me, that means not using herbicides or pesticides, growing plants that support pollinators, being tolerant of and sustaining habitats for birds, insects, and other native creatures that share our space, and generally trying to work with nature, not against her.

My 30-year journey of making this garden and living with plants has been so much fun. There is no destination—we are just part of the process. What I'm grateful for is being part of the continuum of gardeners, stewards of the Earth. I am content with that.

left
On axis to the south border is this flowering crabapple, *Malus transitoria* Golden Raindrops.

EARLY
SPRING

FEBRUARY

I CANNOT UNDERSTAND PEOPLE who put their gardens to bed in October and don't give them another thought until somewhere between St. Patrick's Day and April Fools'. I would like to take them for a walk around my garden in February. At the beginning of the month I could not see a single *Crocus tommasinianus*. By month's end the "tommies" are in full bloom, their lovely shades of lavender to lilac blanketing the hillside. I planted bulbs just once, about 20 years ago, and they did the rest. They are prolific seeders and come up all over the place. I think I bought a hundred bulbs originally—one of my better gardening investments. The deer, squirrels, and chipmunks don't seem to bother them. And even if they wanted to, I think the tommies seed around so readily they could outrun them! Near the barn, the tommies have grown up through the moss, creating a charming scene around a bench. Some people complain that these little crocus get into places where they're not wanted, but I think it's a mark of success in gardening when plants start doing their own thing. It means you've created the right habitat. On a February day when the sun is shining, the tommies open their petals to reveal glowing orange stamens, heralding delights to come. But they don't hang around. By May, the foliage is gone.

The long-awaited and much-anticipated *Galanthus* (snowdrop) season gets into full swing in February. This is a cause of great celebration at the cottage, as snowdrops truly signal the beginning of spring, evoking the opening notes of a symphony that plays out over several months: crocus are the prelude, snowdrops recapitulate the theme, hellebores introduce a variation, and daffodils and tulips are a crescendo.

Simplicity is one of the things I like best about snowdrops. They are not large-flowered or brightly colored, but snowdrops inspire passionate devotion and covetous tendencies. The subtlety and diversity of their flowers is a large part of their appeal—this is one plant that drives me to my knees, to *Look closer!* It's also one of the plants that allows me to say I

above
Crocus tommasinianus comes in wonderful shades of lilac, pink, mauve, and variations thereof.

opposite
Crocus tommasinianus seeds itself wherever it wants, imparting a sense of naturalism.

have something in flower at every season: they start blooming in fall and, depending on the species, go all the way through winter and spring.

In February I tend to like plants that have such moxie that they take whatever nature throws at them and bloom anyway. Despite the continuing threat of frost and snow, they provide food for early pollinators and

are in turn pollinated by them. You may think of this as genetic evolution; I think of it as gambling everything for love. Even though I love the bulbs and perennials that behave this way, you cannot build a garden on a genus or two. You need a variety of plants—including shrubs and trees—to complete the picture we call a garden. Nothing does this so well in late winter and early spring as *Hamamelis ×intermedia* on the tree level and our native *Leucothoe axillaris* on the shrub layer.

Witchhazels—the common name of *Hamamelis* species, because surely some magic must be involved in having them bloom when they do—can take more frost on their blooms than any other tree I know. Certainly the yellow-flowering *H. ×intermedia* 'Arnold's Promise' is the best known, but thanks to the de Belders, Robert and especially his wife Jelena, who was internationally known for her breeding work with the genus over many years at Kalmthout in Belgium, there are many new cultivars and colors from which to choose. I also have *H. ×intermedia* 'Angelly' and 'Pallida', both yellow-flowering. In early spring there's an argument for using lots of yellow, because Mother Nature seems to be working with this color. It's easy to underplant with yellow-marked snowdrops, winter aconites, and hellebores, as well as the yellow-variegated *Carex elata* 'Aurea', yellow-spotted 'Gold Dust' aucuba, and yellow acorus. However, of late I have been expanding my witchhazel collection to include soft reds and oranges, for the same reasons—to create color harmony with the apricot hellebores, *Cornus sanguinea* 'Midwinter Fire' (bloodtwig dogwood), and the bronze fertile fronds of *Matteuccia struthiopteris* (ostrich fern). This makes my color compositions more varied, less monochrome. Among my favorites are *H. ×intermedia* 'Harry', 'Orange Peel', and 'Spanish Spider'; their colors

above
Over winter, the green foliage of *Leucothoe axillaris* gives way to burgundy, which works beautifully with the purples of the tommies.

opposite
Bright yellow of *Hamamelis ×intermedia* 'Angelly'. Witchhazels come in a variety of colors and bloom over several months.

seem easier on the eye. My gaze falls upon the color, as Victorian writers used to say—it doesn't bounce off it, as it might off an acid yellow.

Fragrance is another plus for witchhazels. Few plants at this time of year reward you with such fragrance as you walk by outdoors, and cutting branches for indoor arrangements will help keep your trees manageable in size. Some gardeners fear hamamelis will grow too large for smaller gardens, but judicious pruning is the answer. Wherever the bloom stops on the stalk, I prune it. This is standard cutback pruning, and it will keep trees down to size. There's a little extra work involved in pruning, but it's worth it to have a witchhazel blooming in the landscape

at this time of year. In addition to providing color, fragrance, and beauty indoors and out, this tree has the added bonus of fall foliage color. Definitely a plant for all seasons.

A stroll around the garden late this month shows that the mahonias and *Jasminum nudiflorum* (winter jasmine) are also blooming, along with *Iris reticulata*, *Eranthis hyemalis* (winter aconite), *Chionodoxa* (glory-of-the-snow), and a handful of hellebores. Not only flowers make a statement in the February garden. The bark of some trees is startlingly beautiful, including the exfoliating bark of *Stewartia pseudocamellia*, one of my favorite trees, and *Acer griseum* (paperbark maple). Even the spent flowerheads of hydrangeas, with their antique coloring, have a delicate, lacy quality at this time of year, and of course there are the ever-green trees and shrubs, testament to ongoing life in the garden. Green is one of my favorite colors in any season.

February is also a time for starting seeds, planting up seasonal containers, and doing mundane but essential chores like sharpening tools and cleaning the glass cloches that become decorative elements later in the season. Michael sows seeds of *Lilium formosanum* (Formosa lily) and starts many seeds for the vegetable garden, including sweet peas, which have to soak for a day or so before being sown into long pots (not short ones: sweet peas don't like to have their roots checked). I plan what to sow in the new meadowette; both chicory and poppy seeds require a frost scarification to germinate, so I sow these seeds in situ, just tossing the seeds on the ground or the snow. The snow works with me, pulling the seeds down into the earth. I'm aiming for a different look in the meadow, seasonal waves of color, as though natural populations have seeded up there, one succeeding another. The question is, when to cut the meadow down? It still looks pretty, but you have to take it down so that the new growth can come up. I don't want the old grass there with the new grass coming through, so I cut my meadow by early February. If I wait too long, the early snowdrops will be coming through.

Near a path from the gravel garden down to the cottage, twin containers hewn from tree trunks are planted with *Hamamelis vernalis* 'Quasimodo', a dwarf witchhazel that gets no more than 4 feet tall, underplanted with primroses and *Ophiopogon japonicus* 'Nanum', a mondo grass that grows 6 to 8 inches. Michael created this combination, which makes a really nice seasonal planting. Another 'Quasimodo' may go in the rock garden, and mondo grass among the stones. One of my constant mantras: repetition, repetition, repetition. A classical stone planter in front near the barn stairs picks up the seasonal theme with winter aconites, snowdrops, white-variegated ivy, and some *Arum*

above
All is not done outdoors. Seen here are various forms of *Arum italicum*, which is evergreen.

above right
Hamamelis vernalis 'Quasimodo' is a dwarf witchhazel suitable for both the open garden and containers.

opposite
Classic combination for an arrangement is snowdrops and hamamelis. Both are very fragrant and perfume the air when you bring them into the house.

italicum that has been seeding around the garden. I just dig it up and put it in the pot. Same thing with the aconites—in fact, the container is planted entirely with things from the garden. I added a branch of curly willow to give it a bit of lift. When the aconites and snowdrops are done, we'll dig them out, plant them back in the garden, and put something else in the container. Parts of the garden are constantly in motion—just like nature.

Snowdrops are also featured on one of our taborets, the little stone tables scattered around the garden on which we display still-life vignettes as the fancy takes us. After all, we bring flowers in, or create still-life arrangements in the house. Why not create them outside as well? That's my aim in this book—to blur the lines between indoors and out. Besides, my taborets are another place to celebrate nature. And the wildlife becomes part of it, too. Once, there was a wood thrush eating berries off the stone, and behind that the snowdrops blooming. It was Audubon come to life. This month, a pewter vase shows off snowdrops, flowers of *Hamamelis* ×*intermedia* 'Pallida', and a piece of *Helleborus foetidus* with

just the beginnings of buds. And through the kitchen window, a flower box on the porch displays white-variegated ivy intertwined with the delicate apricot flowers of potted hellebores.

But despite all the variety the February garden has to offer, this month really belongs to snowdrops. When I pull into the driveway late at night from a business trip, my headlights hit the sweep of snowdrops, my little galanthus theater, and I feel I'm home. After hundreds of miles of asphalt, it's a welcoming sight.

So you want to collect snowdrops?

PEOPLE OFTEN SAY that they can't tell snowdrops apart. *Look closer!* Once you can see the differences among them, chances are you'll want to start a collection of your own—perfect for those with obsessive tendencies. As a bonus, you can take great delight in showing off your galanthus blooms to friends in January and February while exclaiming, "Look what's blooming—in January!" Or February. The moment is even more dramatic if there's a little snow on the ground.

A little background: snowdrops are a bulbous genus of plants belonging to the family Amaryllidaceae, which places them on the "not preferred" eating list for deer. All the approximately 20 species are governed by CITES, the Convention on International Trade of Endangered Species of Wild Flora and Fauna; collecting in the wild is forbidden. I'm not going to attempt to describe all 20-some species; I'm just going to acquaint you briefly with three of my favorites.

Galanthus elwesii. Native to Turkey, Greece, Bulgaria, and the Ukraine. Everything about this species (commonly called the giant snowdrop) is big. The many different varieties differ considerably in leaf and flower characteristics. *Galanthus elwesii* and its hybrids have long been favorites of mine. They are usually the first to bloom.

Galanthus nivalis. The most commonly grown species and the one most non-experts associate with the name snowdrop. Its native range is primarily European, especially western and southern Europe. This smaller-flowered snowdrop is among the most widespread, least complicated, and easiest to grow of snowdrops, with many different forms, varieties, and plant heights. There is nothing more beautiful than a large swath of *G. nivalis*, both in the garden and in the woodland. Usually blooms later than *G. elwesii*.

Galanthus plicatus. Native to the Crimean Peninsula, northern Turkey, and Romania. Relatively easy to grow and the only species with distinctive folded foliage. It has large round flowers and makes a good parent plant to many hybrid galanthus. Generally a little later than *G. elwesii*.

Most collectors focus on the unbelievable variety of the cultivated forms. Here are some of my favorite named snowdrops and a stellar base for any collection.

'Ballerina'. This formal semi-double was found in the 1990s by Phil Cornish, a British "immortal" (that is, someone for whom a snowdrop has been named) with a passion for snowdrops and a very keen eye. This one is similar to 'Mrs Wrightson's Double', but on 'Ballerina', the green markings go up only a third of the inner petals. I must confess—I come to most double galanthus with a bit of hesitation; I find their flowers somewhat

awkward, especially when they are irregularly shaped. I much prefer doubles like 'Ballerina', which are so full and regular, they resemble a pompom or a ballerina's tutu.

'Blewbury Tart'. Found in 1975 by renowned English galanthophile Alan Street in a hedgerow in Blewbury, Oxfordshire. Fellow galanthophile John Morley came up with the perfect name: one backstory suggests a person inspired it; another claims the inner green segments look like little tartlets. The flowers are distinctly formed in a symmetrical green rosette. It is easy to grow and increases rapidly. It is a nivalis form—that is, its leaves are flat at the base (applanate) as they emerge from the soil.

'Diggory'. A plicatus, meaning it has recurved margins on the leaf. Usually you have to open a snowdrop to see the inner petals, but the inner green markings on this one are easily seen without opening the outer petals. This is attributable to the length of the claw, the longer part of that outer petal that connects to the ovary (if you think of it as a spoon, it's the handle). Found by Rosie Steele and Richard Hobbs in

above
'Ballerina' is a fine formal semi-double, appealing even to me.

above right
The way 'Blewbury Tart' holds her face up and looks right at you is incredibly cheerful.

a field near Wells in Norfolk, England, around 1993, and named as a memorial to Rosie's son, Diggory Birtles. This snowdrop received the coveted Royal Horticultural Society Award of Garden Merit (AGM).

'E. A. Bowles'. Not only the name of a snowdrop but of an extraordinary British plantsman and author, and also the owner of Myddelton House in Middlesex, England. The snowdrop named for him was found at Myddelton in 2002. It is a beautiful snowdrop with a large flower, all white, poculiform (goblet-shaped), and even, with inners and outers of equal dimensions. It is a fitting tribute to one of my gardening heroes. Yes, this bulb was very expensive, but it now has ten flowers on it. It has increased more than my 401K has. Another AGM winner.

'Godfrey Owen'. This easily recognized snowdrop, a selection of *Galanthus elwesii*, has six outers and six inners in an exquisite cylindrical arrangement. It was found in 1996 by Margaret Owen, a wonderful British galanthophile whom I never saw without a hat. I loved her—she had so much spirit. She named it for her husband. I like the more formal

above
Note how distinctive the outer petals of 'Diggory' are—they are rounded, curved under, and highly textured.

above right
'E. A. Bowles'. My original bulb came from Myddelton House in Middlesex.

double-flowering snowdrops. *Galanthus nivalis* f. *pleniflorus* 'Flore Pleno' is fine for mass plantings, but I do enjoy the refined doubles like 'Godfrey Owen' and 'Ballerina' in my collection. 'Godfrey Owen' has added value for me because of how much I treasured Margaret. A recipient of the RHS Award of Garden Merit.

'Grumpy'. A snowdrop I like for its whimsy. It may not be the most elegant or beautiful snowdrop, but it is distinct, and it makes everyone smile. 'Grumpy' has chubby-looking flowers, a pronounced claw at the base, and broad outer segments. The inside looks like a scowling or frowning face, so you can clearly see how it gets its name. Found in 1990 by plantsman Joe Sharman in Cambridge, England. The vernation (the way the leaves come out of the ground) is supervolute, one tightly clasped around the other.

'Primrose Warburg'. This snowdrop is officially a plicatus (look closely at the leaf, with foliage turning under), but I believe it is a hybrid because the foliage is flat at the base (applanate). It has a yellow ovary and yellow (not the usual green) markings on the inner petals. Its name honors Primrose Warburg, who hosted many a snowdrop luncheon. A year after her 1996 death, galanthophiles gathered to pay her tribute at South Hayes, her garden in England, where they found this very unusual snowdrop. The very similar 'Spindlestone Surprise' is perhaps a little taller.

'Robin Hood'. A personal favorite. Not only do I like the plant, I like the somewhat muddled story behind it: if gardening has taught me one thing, it is to be comfortable in a paradox. British galanthophile James Allen first mentioned this snowdrop in 1891, and the plant was described several times thereafter. Not all those descriptions fit the present-day 'Robin Hood', which resembles a line drawing done by E. A. Bowles in 1948. All stock today is derived from stock distributed by Elizabeth Parker, a galanthophile whose father, R. D. Trotter, received it from Bowles—who did that line drawing. It is tempting to think that it may have come from Bowles' Myddelton House. The flower is rather large, beautifully shaped, and held on a very short pedicel at a jaunty angle. This gives it a distinctive poise. The outers have a long claw that is pointed at the apex. The inner markings look like crossed sabers (hence its name—the plant's legendary namesake was supposed to have done quite a bit of sword fighting). The snowdrop's emerging leaves, like those of many hybrids, are flat in some years, explicative (folded back, seemingly pleated) in others.

'South Hayes'. A very significant and distinctive snowdrop, named in 1992, when it was first seen by visitors to Primrose Warburg's garden in Oxford, England. It has an oblong streak of green on the outer petals, which recurve in the classic pagoda-roof manner. The inner segments are green from the apex to the base, save for the white margins. It too received the RHS Award of Garden Merit.

'Wasp'. One look at its open flower and you can easily see how this snowdrop came by its name. From a distance it looks like a white wasp in flight. The outer petals are long and narrow, and the inner markings suggest a striped thorax. It is a standout in any collection. Found by English galanthophile Veronica Cross in 1995, at Sutton Court in Hertfordshire.

Caring for your galanthus

PEOPLE SAY THAT SNOWDROPS will grow anywhere (except in moist sites), and *Galanthus nivalis* probably will. But if you want optimum results, you'll take care of the soil. Galanthus really appreciate soil that is rich with leaf mold and humus. They do not like wood chips around them. They will grow in part shade to full sun, but they prefer deciduous shade, not evergreen shade. They like well-drained soil. I would never put my more-expensive cultivars into heavy clay.

Conventional wisdom had it that snowdrops be sold or moved "in the green," while they were still growing. But that is a fallacy. The best time is when the bulb is dormant. You can move them in the green, but you must be very careful. If you damage a root, the plant won't grow another root until next season. That being said, when is the best time to take a plant? When you are offered it!

One thing I've learned over the years is to feed snowdrops with half-strength liquid tomato fertilizer after they flower and whenever I move them, to make sure the bulbs have enough nutrients to bulk up and set their flowers for the following year. Most people don't think about feeding snowdrops, but if you have paid a couple hundred dollars for a snowdrop, you are going to take care of it. I realize it's a pain, but it's worth it. Am I doing this every week? No! I feel like I deserve a reward in heaven if I do it once or twice a year. There's ideal and then there's real.

How galanthus grew into a gala

MORE THAN 30 YEARS AGO, Elizabeth Strangman warned me about galanthus. Elizabeth was my hellebore mentor, an internationally known plantswoman who co-wrote a monograph on hellebores and was on the committee for Royal Horticultural Society plant trials. "Beware with snowdrops," she told me, noting that I had an obsessive interest in plants. "They are very addictive." I have found that to be more than true, and my great delight has been to share this love with others. Back then, few people in the United States shared my enthusiasm; fewer than a dozen of us on the East Coast collected snowdrops. In the years since, I have watched the genus approach cult status.

I'm a big champion of winter gardens. Years ago, I led winter-gardening tours to England in February for Winterthur and *Horticulture* magazine. This helped people to see the possibilities of gardening in winter, initially with hellebores—my first passion—and then snowdrops. One of these tours grew into the "Bank to Bend" symposium on winter gardens at

above

An art installation by Gerald Simcoe at the 2019 Galanthus Gala.

above middle

Our longtime friend and gardener extraordinaire Queenie Northrop cheerfully displays one of her snowdrops at the 2019 Galanthus Gala.

above right

International speakers are part of the gala's draw: at left is Valentin Wijnen from Belgium; at right is Tom Mitchell from England. Yours Truly is in the middle.

opposite

A stoneware vase filled with flowering magnolia branches and the graceful racemes and spiky foliage of mahonia celebrates the beauty of early spring.

Winterthur, and now the Galanthus Gala, held each March during the week of the Philadelphia Flower Show.

In 2017, its inaugural year, the gala was an invitation-only affair for a limited number of galanthophiles, but extensive interest turned it public. It now features galanthus growers, juried specialty nursery vendors, and a lecture series by national and international experts. Hundreds of people from all over the United States flock to the gala, which is held at the historic Downingtown Friends Meeting, where I am a member. It is a boutique kind of event where we proudly let our plant geek flag fly. And it's all based on snowdrops. Who would have imagined it, all those years ago?

There are now numerous galanthus collectors, and here and there across North America there are specialists breeding snowdrops, too. Because I love the genus so much, I try to spread the word about the magic of galanthus wherever I go. Occasionally, when I travel to an area that I think isn't sufficiently interested in snowdrops, I've been known to distribute a few bulbs as hostess gifts. I feel like a modern-day Johnny Appleseed!

Forcing spring into flower indoors

I LOVE TO FORCE BRANCHES for winter color indoors. It's rewarding to have flowers and fragrance in the house when nature outside seems frozen—and it's easy to do. You are probably already forcing such plants as narcissus, amaryllis, and tulips to bloom early indoors. Forcing branches significantly increases your winter-defying arsenal. Even before it flowers, a branch can be appreciated for its natural beauty.

In general, ornamental trees and shrubs need 6 weeks of cold winter temperatures before their buds will open, and in our area they usually

have experienced this by February. Indoors, most buds will break dormancy 2 to 4 weeks after you give them warmth and moisture—although this may vary depending on the species. I like to cut my branches on a winter day when the temperature is above freezing. Not only is it easier on the gardener, but the branches are more pliable. It's also the perfect time to do your winter pruning, as you can see where the branches are crossed or misshapen. These prunings are your forcing bounty. Simply cut slender branches to the desired length, and strip off any side growth or leaves that may be below the water line when you use them in an arrangement. Once inside, I submerge the ends of the branches in water and cut them again, underwater, so they start taking up liquid immediately. An older practice among some gardeners was to hit the bottoms of the stems with a hammer. I discourage this because it promotes bacterial growth.

Place the branches in a bucket of water, in a sunny but cool room. Do not place them on or near a heat source, such as a radiator, or you'll cook them. While you are waiting for the buds to open, you must change the water every few days to prevent bacterial growth. For the same reason, I scrupulously clean all containers used for forcing or arrangements, to prevent any bacteria from contaminating future floral adventures.

In addition to being easy and rewarding, forcing branches into bloom is economical. You are getting a lovely display from branches that would be pruned from your trees anyway. I love plants that do double duty, in the garden and again indoors.

Which plants work for forcing? Two of the easiest are pussy willows, which will flower in 2 to 3 weeks, and forsythia, which is even faster. I also recommend *Cornus mas* (Cornelian cherry), *Hamamelis* (witchhazel), flowering quince, PJM rhododendron, amelanchier, magnolia, deutzia, dogwood (it takes about 5 weeks), and *Cercis* (redbud).

In addition to forcing, consider using branches in arrangements year-round. Lindera is beautiful through four seasons as a cut branch. Try a branch of fig, or wisteria. Just about any branch in bud, flower, or fruit is suitable, and even bare branches can add charm or drama to an arrangement.

above
Just a few days of warm weather will bring *Cornus mas* into bloom after you bring branches indoors. Cut them when they are in bud.

opposite
Cercis chinensis f. *alba* makes an elegant addition to a monochromatic arrangement, combined with white tulips or white iris.

From garden to kitchen

JUST ABOUT EVERY REGION of the world has its favorite dishes, and the Pennsylvania Dutch region of Pennsylvania, where I spent my early childhood, is no exception. The early settlers to this area—who weren't Dutch at all, but Europeans from various localities who spoke a version of *Deutsch* (German)—brought with them many traditions, including traditional ways of preparing the fruits and vegetables they grew in this new land. Michael and I are both of Pennsylvania Dutch heritage. Our families were among those early settlers, having arrived in Philadelphia in the late 1600s and early 1700s. Generation after generation, they passed along a love of the land and what it could provide. Not all made their livings from farming, but there was an innate sense of their agrarian roots. Mike's father and grandfather made their livings from the earth, and I spent summers with my maternal grandparents, John and Irene Thorpe, who had a farm in the foothills of Tennessee's Great Smoky Mountains. I would take the train from Reading Terminal in Philadelphia and be picked up at the station in Knoxville.

That connection to the earth provided a rhythm to life. I can remember going with my grandparents to friends' houses for seed swaps, opening the little tin boxes in which they kept the seeds and sharing them around. Heirloom beans and peas were especially prized. And I watched my grandparents and their friends and families come together to pick the produce and can it. It was part of the fabric of the community that I hope is never lost—plants and food bringing people together.

I like to think that everything has a purpose, even plants we think of as weeds. Plants, after all, have been used in a multitude of different

ways over the centuries—for medicines, for perfumes and deodorizers, for bedding, for decorating our dwellings. But primarily for food. Foragers today are relearning what our ancestors knew, that many weeds are really wild foods. Rampant, thug-like ostrich ferns are transformed into tasty fiddleheads on the plate. Scorned dandelions, which escaped into the wild after being brought to this country for culinary purposes, can reclaim their original purpose as a salad. Weedy sorrel can be harvested to make a delicious soup.

Cooking is part of our heritage, and being able to grow even a part of what I bring to my table enriches any meal. So do pass-along recipes from family and friends. Most of the recipes featured in this book highlight food from our garden or our community, and several are recipes that evoke warm memories of the people who shared them. Some trace directly back to our Pennsylvania Dutch roots. Most of them were prepared by Michael—I'm not as good a cook as he is, because I'm always running out into the garden while things are on the stove.

A lot of gardeners are excellent cooks, and I've often wondered how they manage it, especially if they have big gardens. My friend and gardening mentor Joanna Reed often prepared wonderful meals for large groups, and British gardener Christopher Lloyd was renowned for his skill in the kitchen. I was walking with him in his garden one day when I heard a timer go off; I thought perhaps it signalled that my time was up, that maybe he had something else going on. But he pulled a kitchen timer out of his pocket, excused himself, and off he went inside. A little later, as we continued our walk, the timer went off a second time, and the same thing happened—and I finally got it! The alarms were reminders to tend to what he was cooking. I'm not sure how I feel about cell phones in the garden in general, but their alarms are especially handy for people like me, who so easily lose track of time in the garden. I'll go out for a few minutes with a cup of coffee, and three hours later I'm still out there, cutting things back or weeding, whatever was on the stove completely forgotten.

Whatever it takes, I hope you will try out some of the recipes we share in the following pages, or recipes that are part of your own family's history. Use some ingredient you have grown yourself, even if it's just an herb from a pot on your window sill. Being aware of how plants enhance your life is one of the best seasonings you can add to any dish.

above
The vegetable garden feeds you both spiritually and literally. Many of these vegetables from the spring harvest end up on our table.

COEUR *à la* CRÈME

If ever a dessert was made for Valentine's Day, it's this one. What could be more romantic than a delicious "heart of cream" floating in a lake of red liqueur-tinged fruit sauce?

There are many variations of this classic French dessert, but this recipe comes from our friend Queenie Northrop, who has traditionally made this dessert for Valentine's Day dinner parties.

INGREDIENTS

8 oz cream cheese at
    room temperature

1¼ cups heavy cream

⅔ cup powdered sugar

1 vanilla bean

1 tbsp lemon juice

1 tsp baking soda

2 packages of frozen
    raspberries, each
      6 oz, for sauce

Fresh raspberries for garnish

3 tbsp Crème de Cassis

Ice water

Cheesecloth

Heart-shaped mold

METHOD

Mix ice water with the baking soda and lemon juice, then soak the cheesecloth in the water until it is saturated and cold. Wring out the cheesecloth. Line the heart-shaped mold with the damp cheesecloth, with enough overlap to cover mixture later.

Whip the heavy cream in a bowl until peaks form, then add the powdered sugar and continue whipping until soft peaks return. Set aside.

Scrape the seeds from the vanilla bean into a bowl with the cream cheese, and whip until light and fluffy. Fold the heavy cream and the cream cheese mixtures together.

Spoon the mixture into the mold on top of the cold cheesecloth. Smooth the surface, then fold the overlap cheesecloth over the top so the mixture is covered. Refrigerate overnight.

To make the raspberry sauce, puree the frozen raspberries with the Crème de Cassis, then strain through a sieve. Chill.

When ready to serve, remove heart mold from refrigerator, fold back top layers of cheesecloth, and carefully invert mold onto a presentation plate. Carefully remove remaining cheesecloth from the heart-shaped dessert. Drizzle raspberry sauce on the plate around the heart so it is sitting in a pool of red sauce. Add drizzle of sauce to heart, if desired, and garnish with fresh whole raspberries. Serve immediately.

opposite
Coeur à la Crème is a perfect treat
for you and your valentines.

MARCH

I ALWAYS LOOK FORWARD to March. Despite the rewards in the garden at this time of the year, it can be a very cruel month—perhaps the most heart-wrenching of the season. We think we know what to expect in other months. March is unpredictable. Sometimes it's warm, sometimes it's cool, and sometimes those precious flowers that you've waited for all year long are ruined by snow. Yet I love March!

Recent years have been particularly challenging. Very cool springs and Nor'easters have made it difficult for the gardener. However, this weather can be a boon for hellebores, galanthus, and most other early bulbs, because the cooler temperatures make the flowers last longer. So despite the challenges, there is a positive side—more time to savor these usually fleeting moments in the garden. And you learn to appreciate every sunny day so much more!

Convention says the well-loved daffodils are the signature bulb for March and April. This month, they share the stage with hellebores, which play a starring role.

I have been growing hellebores in my garden for over 30 years. I'm so identified with them that a friend gave me a T-shirt emblazoned *Born to raise HELLEBORES*. The moment I saw them, it was love at first sight. I was gardening in a suburb of Charlotte, North Carolina, at the time; I had bought an antebellum house whose previous owner was a breeder of camellias. One February morning I was looking at a camellia and noticed a large clump of pale pink hellebores in full bloom at the base of the bush. A shaft of sunlight was shining directly on it. I felt like this was a message from above, and I knew I was forever in love. For me, the time of the year in which they bloom would have been reason enough. No matter what Mother Nature throws at them, hellebores keep on blooming. They withstand frost and late snows. I usually only worry about them when temperatures reach the low 20s. When I'm suffering from chlorophyll withdrawal, they are one of my sure cures—along with snowdrops and daffodils. But it was also the color possibilities hellebores afforded that simply blew me away.

My first trip to Germany to learn more about them changed my life. There I met Gunther Yogel, who was growing them as cut flowers for Valentine's Day. It was the early 1990s, and so many of the colors and forms I was seeing were not available in the United States—but I knew I had to have them. In Europe and especially in England, when I admired a plant, aficionados kindly offered me a division, the caveat being that I had to return a year or two later to pick it up. This impracticality led me to the idea of breeding my own, and I applied for my U.S. Department of Agriculture import license.

The year after I traveled to Germany, I visited Elizabeth Strangman in England. Elizabeth was the owner of Washfield Nursery, a well-respected nursery in Kent, and her eye for distinctive plants was one of the best I have encountered anywhere in the world. She taught me how to judge a flower as well as how she did her breeding work. She also introduced me to John Massey, owner of Ashwood Nurseries in the West Midlands, and many other breeders. Over the next several years, hellebore breeding began to take off in the United States, and a core group of breeders developed, including Northwest Garden Nursery in Oregon, which produces the Winter Jewels series, and Pine Knot Farms in Virginia, which has Pine Knot Hellebores. I developed my own strain, Brandywine Hellebores, here at the cottage, so when you see these plants, you know where they came from—I bred them, selected them, crossed them, harvested the seed, and tended them for many years.

The names of my hellebores are meant to reflect a certain time in the garden. Brandywine Hellebore 'Evening Mist' captures the late afternoon, verging on evening, when the light starts to look misty; Brandywine 'Sunrise' is a name that needs no explanation. I don't plant my hellebores in solid blocks of color, because that is not what nature does. I situate them so that other plants echo and highlight them—an apricot one under an apricot quince, for example. It's more in the cottage style. I feel that heavy color blocks would be too modern, or too controlled, for the style of our garden.

above
Brandywine Hellebores color offerings. My goal in breeding them was to expand the palette of possibilities. Think of me as the crayon man, if you will, adding to the number of colors in the box.

opposite
Clockwise from top left: *Athyrium niponicum* var. *pictum*; an unnamed polygonatum from a collection trip to Japan; Brandywine Hellebore 'Evening Mist'.

In recent years the exciting breeding work has continued. Some of the most beautiful and unique color work comes from Thierry Delabroye in France and Ashwood Nurseries in England. Many other nurseries in Europe and the United States, including Marietta and Ernie O'Byrne's Northwest Garden Nursery in Oregon, have also produced stellar strains. I'm glad to see improvements in this genus that I love. But I still think that one of the most important attributes for any plant—hellebores or anything else—is how it performs in the garden. The success of a plant doesn't rest just on aesthetics but on function as well. I tend to use the species and the orientalis hybrids in the woodland, where I think they look more naturalistic, and the interspecific hybrids in the garden. It's just a matter of personal interpretation.

Getting the best from your hellebores

SOMEONE ASKED ME if I minded the fact that hellebores face downward. I replied no, and then I asked whether they thought there was room in this world for plants you had to touch to enjoy fully. Perhaps that is part of the charm of hellebores—they are participatory plants. (But note, as you turn up those nodding flowers to admire their faces: all parts of hellebore plants are poisonous, so wash your hands after handling them for any reason.) Many plants in the family Ranunculaceae—to which hellebores belong—nod downward on cold, cloudy, or rainy days, and upward on sunny days. It's easy to see why a lot of early bloomers do this: it's to protect themselves. If these plants held their flowers face-up, they would be ruined on snowy, sleety days. However, my personal preference is for outward-facing flowers, because you can see them more readily. That's also why I like growing hellebores on hillsides and banks.

You may think of the hellebore flower as having petals. In fact, those "petals" are actually sepals—protective parts of the plant. Sepals want to be green, or greenish, but over the

above

The hillside garden puts the
hellebores at eye-level, the better
to look up into their nodding
flowers. If you don't have a hillside,
use them in a window box or potted
as a tabletop centerpiece where
you can appreciate the blooms.

opposite

I've planted hellebores throughout
my one-acre hillside garden almost
as a ground cover.

centuries they developed color to attract pollinators. It has taken years
of breeding to make clearer colors, away from the natural greenish
tendency. Hellebores now come in every color of the rainbow except true
blue or true red. There are double, single, and anemone forms. So many
choices. People ask me which ones they should have, and my answer is
simple: you should have them all.

Hellebores come in two basic groups. Caulescent hellebores, including *Helleborus foetidus*, *H. lividus*, *H. argutifolius*, and *H. vesicarius*, have
flowers and leaves on one stem. Acaulescent hellebores produce flowers
and leaves on separate stems. Knowing this distinction is important: if
you cut the stem on caulescent types while tidying up foliage, you lose the
flower; and if you are breeding hellebores, it's best to do crossings within
a group, as in caulescent with caulescent.

Please, for the love of all things holy, remove the dead leaves from your hellebores so they won't detract from new buds and flowers. I always remove the previous year's foliage, starting early in the new year—sometimes later, if we get a lot of snow. The flowers are presented

above
Double hellebores come in all the color forms that are available in the singles. Again, the choice is yours, but my preference is always for un-muddied colors.

above middle
Of the many species, one of the easier ones to find and to grow is *Helleborus foetidus*.

above right
A hellebore taboret that also features quail eggs and a vintage watering can. Hellebores can be used as cut flowers; simply replace the ones that flag.

opposite
Hellebores team up with heuchera, carex, and bloodtwig dogwood in this container, a study in textures as well as color.

better without the distraction of tatty old leaves. This trimming has to be done before the new hellebore buds appear, as it's much more difficult to cut around them. It's a sickening feeling to cut off a bud because you are in a hurry—similar to slicing a bulb in half with a trowel because you've forgotten where you planted it. Removing the leaves is also a good way to minimize disease. Don't put the old leaves in the compost, however; they take several years to decay, and you don't want to create fungal problems.

Hellebores grow best in part shade (they will live in dense shade but will not bloom well, or at all), and they really hate soggy soils or overly wet sites. Don't plant the crowns too deep; I keep the crown right at ground level. Properly sited, they are easy to grow and long-lived; I have left clumps undivided in my garden for 20 years. They bloom from March until I cut the flowers off at the end of May for their seed. How many plants give you three months of flowers? I also use hellebores in containers and as cut flowers in arrangements, and I often float the flowers in bowls—just as my mother and grandmother floated camellias and pansies.

Propagating hellebores

HELLEBORES CAN BE PROPAGATED sexually or asexually. Sexual propagation uses traditional pollination methods. Hellebore flowers are able to self-pollinate, but nature discourages this. The stigmas, or female parts of the flower, usually are receptive before the stamens are ready to release pollen, which encourages cross-fertilization. I do not emasculate my plants (that is, remove the male parts). I will often take the flower that will provide the pollen into the house and float it in a dish of water, because the heat indoors makes the pollen vessel dehisce (or open) faster. I then transfer the pollen outdoors to my female parent. I don't use a brush to apply it—I would need a separate brush for each plant, because old pollen may stick to the brush. Instead, I use a ballpoint pen to transfer pollen, as you can clean it off easily. I do this cross three days running, to prevent any other pollen from entering and also to preclude self-pollination.

I collect the seeds when they are ripe, in May. When sowing the seed—which I recommend doing immediately after gathering it, or within a few weeks—I barely cover it with soil. The seeds usually germinate after a few frosts, and the plants will bloom three years later. You can speed up this cold stratification process by using refrigeration to manipulate the temperatures of seeds and plants. (In other words, instead of allowing the plants to go through a natural year's cycle, you can put them in a refrigerator and let them chill to simulate another winter. This process can cut the time by as much as a year.)

Asexual propagation by division is easy, and you are assured of creating a plant that is identical to your parent plant. The optimal time to do this is in late summer, when the flower buds have already been produced. However, I would divide a plant in spring, knowing that it may not bloom for another year. Instead, the plant will put its energy into making roots. I dig up the plant I want to divide, loosen the soil and knock off any excess, then try to get at least two leaves and some old roots on each division. After washing off the soil, you usually can see quite clearly where the divisions should be made. I tend to make my divisions rather large, because I like the look of an established clump, but you can make your divisions as small as the plant dictates—where the individual crowns are. If you are trying to make up numbers of a particular plant, smaller divisions may work for you. If the ground is dry, you have to water regularly until the plants become established. Once established, they don't need much attention.

But which hellebores do you want more of? Your first consideration, I think, is to choose a flower that appeals to you. Is it the shape? The color? Both are important. I prefer that all the petals, or sepals, be uniform: whether star-shaped or cup-shaped, in my opinion they all should be the same. Color too is a matter of personal taste. I prefer saturated color or color patterns—contrasting eye zones or nectaries, evenly distributed freckled or spotty patterns. Interestingly, hellebores begin to fade after pollination. I happen to like this. The colors remind me of old linens or antique fabrics.

"Gardening" in the barn

IT ISN'T QUITE SPRING in the barn, although as I entered one chilly March morning recently the notes of Copland's *Appalachian Spring* were washing over the plants within. But it isn't quite winter, either, inside this old circa-1790 carriage barn. It's like a little world of its own, where music plays constantly from an all-classical station. This is where scores of tender plants brought in from the garden while away the coldest months in a semi-suspended state. We keep the temperature on the cool side (45 to 50 degrees Fahrenheit); I don't want things to grow in here, I just want them to live. And I use six panels of lights, alternating fluorescent and grow bulbs for the best light frequency.

I feel a bit like I'm in the ark in here, with all the plants crowded in. Birdhouses that have suffered injury of some kind line the walls. They are the casualties of time, but a year or two ago a pair of wrens moved into one of the houses and spent the winter living in the barn. I don't know how they moved in and out, but I tried not to spook them. I considered it their space, too. They were in a garden of sorts, with some plants happily in pots, like my tender oak and the Meyer lemons, and others, such as the bananas and the colocasias, dormant until they move outside again. Stacked on floor and benches are numerous other plants not hardy in our zone 7: geraniums,

above
With spring imminent, I set up my seedling trays to get a jump on the gardening season. I cannot resist watching the plants push through the earth.

phormiums, clivias, crinums, echeverias and other succulents, olives, lavenders, rosemary, acanthus, melianthus, ferns, manfredas, and a selection of different agaves. There's also *Ficus afghanistanica* 'Silver Lyre', a wild fig from Afghanistan with lovely silvery leaves, and the endangered *Araucaria angustifolia*, whose seeds are a delicacy in its native South America. This whole area of the barn speaks of texture.

Then there's the *Prunus mume* (Japanese flowering apricot) I acquired when I was lecturing at the Atlanta Botanical Garden years ago. It's *P. mume* 'Beni-chidori', and I first saw it in England in Lady Mary Keen's garden. She had it growing on a wall (she thought it was more tender than some), and its flowers were a richer color than any I had seen, a more saturated dark pink, with lavender overtones. I was on the trail of that plant for ten years, so when I saw it in Atlanta, I used part of my honorarium to buy it. But I couldn't get it onto the plane when I flew home. It was too big. So I gave it to my sister, who lives in Nashville, and she took it home to babysit until I could retrieve it. She really didn't want to: she was afraid she would kill it. A year later, I decided to bring it home. I took it to a UPS center, where they had to make a special box. In the end, it cost more to ship it than it did to buy it, which shows what lengths collectors will go to just to get *that* plant!

I grow 'Beni-chidori' in a pot, but perhaps one day we'll find a place for it to grow outside. Meanwhile, I drag it inside and out again with the change of the seasons. But every time I look at it, I understand why the Japanese have festivals around these plants. If I could, I'd have every *Prunus mume* I could get my hands on. Unfortunately, not all are hardy. When you have them outside, because they bloom so early, they'll often bloom for a week—or even a few days—and then get blasted by cold weather. It reminds me to appreciate beauty wherever I see it, no matter how fleeting. That's what makes it precious.

above

My old barn, a suitable greenhouse substitute, is packed to the rafters with plants. This view through the French doors shows just a few of the more than 90 pots that are winter residents.

Delighting in daffodils

WHEN I WAS STILL IN COLLEGE, daffodils were my first cure for an acute case of winter-induced cabin fever. I gathered armloads of them for my apartment and would have them everywhere–in glasses, in jars, in vases. The mass effect of daffodils both indoors and out was overwhelming. I knew little then about the intricacies of plant collecting–but perhaps daffodils were my gateway plant to hellebores and galanthus. They bloomed before tulips, and I thought every one in the world belonged to me.

Daffodils are much loved, and commonly thought of as yellow, although recent breeding work has produced them in greens, oranges, pinks, and combinations thereof. And where once convention held that daffodils were yellow and narcissus had white petals, they do

hybridize readily, and the terms are now generally used interchangeably. Scientifically, however, the common daffodil is *Narcissus pseudonarcissus*, in the family Amaryllidaceae.

Daffodils grow for years in clumps with little or no care. I think most look best with a background of green leaves, whether they are in the garden or in arrangements. They *definitely* look better not planted in rows. Drifts are much preferred. I am always happy when I see them growing under trees, on grassy banks, along driveways, or even in the grass as I drive through the countryside. Sometimes they are just memories of a garden long gone and the gardener who tended it. I am grateful for their floral legacy.

For mass effect here at the cottage, I use 'Ice Follies' daffodils. I have lots of them, with their white petals and yellow cups, at the bottom of the hillside, but as you look up the hill you're likely to see more of the bright yellow 'King Alfred'. Daffodil snobs sometimes turn up their noses at 'King Alfred', one of the most widely grown daffodils, but putting that stronger color further away attracts your gaze up and back. It's the same idea as putting forsythia at the top of the hill—its vivid yellow draws the eye upward without putting a "Hollywood" sign up there. In addition to these stalwarts, I like the species and old-fashioned narcissus/daffodils. These include the creamy 'W. P. Milner' with its graceful swan neck, an attribute that many people dislike. I do like it: I think its look better suits a naturalistic garden. I often use my collectible daffodils in meadows or along pathways, where one can appreciate the nuances.

Daffodils are divided into 13 divisions, mostly according to flower shape. 'King Alfred' is in Division 1 (trumpets); 'Ice Follies' is in Division 2 (large-cupped); other favorites are the jonquilla types of Division 7, most of which have more than one flower to their rounded stems. I love the early-blooming varieties usually found in Division 6 (cyclamineus daffodils) and the very last-blooming poeticus cultivars of Division 9,

above
Narcissus 'W. P. Milner' has the graceful form of a species, an apparent "wildling" in the garden.

opposite
Narcissus 'April Queen' (1938) has long-lasting bloom.

clearly reminiscent of *Narcissus poeticus*, which start in late February and are still blooming in May.

Once a daffodil leaf is damaged, it is done for and cannot be replaced. Many tidy gardeners like to keep the leaves neat by tying them in knots or braids, or folding them in two and putting an elastic band around them. No doubt this practice makes the garden look tended, but the effect on the bulb is disastrous. If you leave the foliage alone, and tolerate it for the few weeks during which it looks less than architectural, you will be rewarded with a superior display the following spring. I don't do anything with mine other than pushing the foliage gently aside, without damaging it, to prevent the leaves from falling over onto other plants. As time permits, I do deadhead old flowers. This is not necessary, but it does enable the plant to put more energy into the bulb, rather than trying to make seed. It's just a little thing that helps the bulbs live longer. I remove the old foliage when the leaves are yellow and starting to decay—usually when I can pull them off with my hands without cutting.

In the garden, avoid planting the bulbs too deep, as this may cause them to deplete their resources as they try to get out of the ground to reach light for photosynthesis. On the other hand, if you plant them too shallow, it may expose the bulbs to temperature extremes. This may cause a bulb to divide and split, which is good for propagation but bad for bloom, as it takes time to develop to flowering size. The general rule for planting is to dig a hole twice the height of the bulb. If there is any doubt, I usually err on the shallower side.

Happily, daffodils are deer resistant. If you have pets, don't put bone meal in the hole. It will encourage not only your pets but also squirrels and other wild critters to dig up the bulbs. Leaf mold is my answer to everything. It's the natural thing to do. After all, what does the forest give back? Its leaves. But I do grind them up before I put them on the garden. Bulbs are planted in the fall, of course. I usually plant well into December, until the ground freezes.

above
A charming little daffodil with an unfortunate name: *Narcissus* 'Xit'.

opposite
Narcissus poeticus is one of the last daffodils to bloom in my garden.

DANDELION SALAD *with* HOT BACON DRESSING

INGREDIENTS

4 cups dandelion (or endive) greens, cleaned and chopped

6 slices bacon

2 or 3 hard-boiled eggs for garnish

1½ tbsp flour

2 tbsp sugar

1 tsp salt

1 egg

¼ cup vinegar

2 cups milk

Dandelion Salad is like the sautéed fiddlehead ferns of April—you can enjoy these dishes only in spring. Both are seasonal delicacies and require prompt harvesting of the main ingredient.

Gather nutrient-rich dandelions (Taraxacum officinale) *while the leaves are still small and tender, before the flowers emerge. Older, larger leaves can be bitter. (If you do end up with a lot of dandelion flowers, you can always dip them in batter to make fritters.) Make sure you know what you are picking, as even such well-known weeds as dandelions have some look-alikes. Dandelion leaves are hairless and saw-toothed. As always, it is safest to eat dandelions gathered from your own organic garden or lawn. If you collect them in the wild, stay away from any areas that might have been sprayed with herbicides or pesticides, such as along roadways or railway tracks, or any area where the plants might have absorbed pollutants. If you don't have your own dandelions, you can often find organically grown dandelion greens at farmers' markets or some specialty food stores. Or you can substitute endive greens.*

This recipe for Dandelion Salad with Hot Bacon Dressing is from Michael's grandmother, Mrs. Jacob Alderfer.

METHOD

Hard-boil the eggs for the garnish, cool and peel. Rinse dandelion leaves in cold water and pat dry with paper towels, or clean them in a lettuce spinner, before chopping to desired size. Place in serving bowl.

To make the dressing, mix together the flour, sugar, and salt. Add egg, vinegar, and milk, and stir until well blended. In a pan, fry the bacon until crisp, remove from drippings, and put to one side. Add dressing mixture to drippings in the pan, stir, and cook until thickened. Cool slightly, then pour over dandelion greens and mix. Garnish with sliced hard-boiled eggs and crumbled bacon.

opposite
Dandelion Salad with Hot Bacon Dressing is the traditional Pennsylvania Dutch dandelion salad, often found at church socials or family dinners in early spring.

DANDELION SALAD
(vegetarian style)

For those who prefer their dandelions unadorned with bacon or hard-boiled eggs, this simple salad should hit the spot. It features tender young dandelion leaves for an early spring treat, but baby spinach can be substituted at other times of the year. The recipe also calls for garlic scapes, the stalks that grow from the bulbs of hardneck garlic plants in spring; they are tender, with a milder flavor than the garlic bulb, and are often available at farmers' markets in spring. If none are available, try substituting chives or scallion greens to taste.

INGREDIENTS

8 cups fresh young dandelion
    leaves, torn into pieces

1 tbsp finely chopped
    garlic scapes

¼ cup extra-virgin olive oil

1 tbsp fresh lemon juice

½ tsp coarse sea salt

¼ tsp granulated sugar

METHOD

In a small bowl, combine garlic scapes, lemon juice, salt, and sugar, and whisk to combine well. Drizzle the olive oil into the bowl in a slow stream, whisking until emulsified.

Place the dandelion leaves in a salad bowl. Drizzle the dressing over the greens, and toss to coat. Serve immediately.

opposite
This vegetarian dandelion salad is my favorite. Dandelions were brought over from the Old World as a food crop but escaped from gardens. Our sweet revenge is to eat them.

LATE SPRING

APRIL

APRIL HAS TRADITIONALLY been associated with gentle showers, blue skies, and sunshine without scorching. Lately, the month is much more capricious. April showers bring May flowers, so the saying goes. But a late freeze or a dry April seems to be just about the worst that can happen to spring. Or is it just that we have such high expectations of this month? Certainly a cool April extends the bloom time of the bulbs and the spring ephemerals. But an April that brings a series of 90-plus days wrecks every flowering daffodil, tulip, magnolia, and spring ephemeral in a matter of hours, or, at best, days.

As a child, before I knew the joys of winter gardening with snowdrops and hellebores, my idea of paradise must have been April. I could be outside in the garden, or exploring the woodlands among the flowering dogwoods and redbuds. And when their bloom times overlapped, well... heaven. The color and the light seemed different to me. Perhaps it was merely the shade of green on the emerging leaves–fresh, often chartreuse, which has always been one of my favorite colors. It was, and still is, just beautiful.

As the trees bloom, they add more colors to that layer of the garden– crabapples, halesias, magnolias, along with the dogwoods and redbuds. If you are doing spatial layering in the garden, you can see the tree layer more clearly now, because it is defined by color. And you can bring the color down to the shrub layer, because that's also blooming, and even further down, to the lower, ephemeral level. I see hepaticas and anemonellas (*Thalictrum thalictroides*) in bloom early in April. I grow both white- and pink-flowered anemonellas. Years ago, I came across them in my walks in the woods, so I put them in my garden, trying to erase another line, the one between wild and cultivated spaces. Truth be told, few places have escaped the hand of man, and it is through these walks on the wild side that I find the most inspiration for my garden–and the greatest sense of healing for my soul, for that matter. The green mosses combined

with the unfurling crozures of ferns emphasize the great delicacy and tenacious nature of plants willing to live after a cold winter. Large drifts of *Mertensia virginica* bloom in low-lying places in an explosion of blue. I started out with a small drift of these Virginia bluebells in my garden, and it is slowly increasing, even though my garden has tended toward dry over the years.

Trilliums, well loved and easily recognized, are the highlight of spring wildflowers. Words like *magical* and *ethereal* come to mind when I see them blooming in the garden and in the wild. The 48 species are native to North America and to Asia; 35 occur on our continent, the bulk of them in the South. These typically woodland plants fall into two groups: pedicellate (flowers borne on a stem above the leaves) and sessile (flowers set directly on the leaves). In his *Species Plantarum*, published in 1753, Carl Linnaeus, father of binomial nomenclature, established the genus *Trillium* based on three American species. They hold a special place in my heart, as they are one of the first wildflowers I learned to recognize on woodland walks with my grandparents and friends in the Great Smoky Mountains.

Not only are they special to me, they are special to many others, inspiring an almost cult-like devotion. Thousands flock to the Spring Wildflower Pilgrimage in Great Smoky Mountains National Park every year, where trilliums are among the attractions. Also in spring, you can visit one of the world's premier collections of trilliums at Mt. Cuba Center in Hockessin, Delaware, a botanical garden known for its

above
Emerging foliage. From left:
Paeonia lactiflora; *Rosa*; *Hydrangea arborescens* 'Annabelle'.

above
Combinations on the tree
layer: *Magnolia* 'Elizabeth', *M.
×soulangeana*, *M.* 'Marjory Gossler'.

woodland gardens and preservation and propagation of native plants. Trilliums grow in neutral to alkaline soil; they are average in difficulty of culture, and the time to divide them is as they go dormant. Deer do browse them, as they do most plants in the Liliaceae, but habitat degradation is the main reason that certain species are threatened. Since we contributed to the problem, shouldn't we help address it by planting more trilliums in our gardens?

In April, the bulb layer is in full swing. Daffodils bloom very early in the month, tulips in late April and early May, and fritillarias, like precious gems, add to the show all month. As gardeners become more bulb-minded, as they learn how eager bulbs are to please and what interest they offer to the garden, they add more of them to their gardens. Tulips, daffodils, fritillarias, muscari, scilla, chionodoxa, galanthus,

alliums, lilies—the list is endless. Bulbs bring immeasurable value and a certain depth to your planting style, and you can bring the outdoors in with armfuls of their colorful blooms. And summer "bulbs" (caladium, colocasia, calla lilies, freesias, ranunculus, crocosmia, tuberous begonias) can be planted now, in spring, for flowers or foliage in summer or fall; they are excellent for filling in when flowering plants begin to falter.

But even bulbs require some effort. This is the time of year when I start pulling the spent flowers off the daffodils. This helps the overall strength of the bulb (no energy wasted on making seed), and it looks better too, allowing you to see the hellebores again. I do this just a little bit at a time, not all at once. I also go around taking old flowers off the hydrangeas. I like to leave them on through the winter, when they still look lacy, but now I think they are just distracting. You owe it to yourself to do these chores. You could think of it as still picking flowers, except now they're spent.

Each year, we plant hundreds of tulips of all kinds and colors in the cutting garden, and we use bright orange tulips in the roadside bed to stop traffic—or at least slow it down as the road curves past our property. But the tulips in the borders are predominantly white and black (well, *Tulipa* 'Queen of Night' is a deep velvety maroon that reads as black). Elsewhere I have the lovely white viridiflora 'Spring Green', which has done so well for me that I've decided to try pink and yellow varieties (all viridiflora tulips have green feathering). Originally, 'Spring Green' was chosen as a color echo for the green eye and white

above
Trilliums are a quintessential American wildflower. From left: *Trillium erectum*; *T. luteum*; *T. flexipes*.

opposite
Fritillaria persica. Fritillarias are suitable for rock gardens and front of borders. They appreciate well-drained soils.

bracts of *Cornus florida*, one of my favorite understory trees, which went with the white cottage, the white picket fence, and, from a different angle, the white bells of *Halesia carolina*. The original dogwoods have since succumbed to anthracnose and been replaced with the more disease-resistant *C. florida* 'Appalachian Spring'. I can never get enough dogwoods. I think that *C. florida* and *Magnolia grandiflora* are probably the best two ornamental trees that America has given the world. These two New World plants are used all over Europe for their visual appeal.

Halesias, with their stunning white bell-shaped flowers, are a magnet for bees and other pollinators when they bloom in April. There are always tons of insects on my *Halesia carolina* (silverbell), which is native to the Southeast, including the mountains of Appalachia, where I spent much of my childhood. But my first memory of halesia—that aha! moment when I realized I had to have it—is linked to Independence Hall in Philadelphia. Years ago, when the Pennsylvania Horticultural Society's offices were located in that area, a couple of silverbells were growing nearby. I thought what an elegant tree it was, and then I found out it was native. For just a few days each year, my halesia scatters its petals on the pathway by the barn, and it is magical. It's one of my favorite places to sit, if I ever get time to sit.

This month, buds are showing on a dwarf form of *Crataegus monogyna* (English hawthorn), which I've had for about 15 years. This tree is not easy to grow in my garden. Years ago, when I was the "celebrated garden expert" at a garden fair at Ladew Topiary Gardens, an interviewer asked me to name my favorite plant there. My usual response is to name the plant I'm standing next to, and I happened to be standing beside this. Well, they gave it to me as a thank-you gift, and when I got it home I wondered what I would do with just one. So I ordered three more—from the only

nursery in the United States that grew it, which was in Oregon. A year after the three trees arrived at the cottage, two died. Of course, I had to get two more sent over, the last two the nursery had. It's a beautiful plant with little white flowers. But when you consider the lengths I went to so I could grow it, it's a lesson in how a blithe comment can cost you a lot of money!

Winter hazels (*Corylopsis*) are among the plants demanding center stage this month. I have several different varieties of these multi-stemmed shrubs, which feature delightfully drooping clusters of golden, bell-shaped flowers. Visitors may wonder why I have a forsythia nearby, and think that the design would be better without it. But it is a variegated forsythia that picks up the yellow—and in designing a garden you have to think beyond the immediate moment. What's going to happen two months from now? You won't notice the corylopsis once the flowers are gone, but you will take note of the variegated forsythia. Variegation, as long as you don't overdo it, is a useful accent, and foliage and texture are important for maintaining year-round interest.

As you walk around the garden you have different experiences color-wise, but I often use yellow or purple to tie borders and peripheral areas together. In the gold border on the south side of the garden I have the variegated daylily *Hemerocallis* 'Lemon Splash', *Carex elata* 'Aurea' (Bowles' golden sedge), and a gold-variegated Solomon's seal. I like *Hakonechloa macra* 'All Gold' as a vertical element in the rose pillar border, and also because I've found it will take more sun than any other hakone grass. I saw

the straight species growing wild in Japan years ago, on a streambank, so I knew it liked moist but well-drained soil. Here also is *Geranium phaeum* var. *phaeum* 'Samobor', which was given to me by Elizabeth Strangman, who found it near the town of Samobor in Croatia; this weedy selection picks up on the purple I use around the garden, such as the purple tulips and the potted phormiums. I never had to worry about the back of this border because it was covered with trees, but then they all came down in an ice storm several years ago. I now have a crabapple (*Malus transitoria* Golden Raindrops) and a redbud (*Cercis canadensis* 'Tennessee Pink'), along with our native pinkshell azaleas (*Rhododendron vaseyi*) and a row of peonies to provide cut flowers for the house.

In the jewel box garden on the north side of the cottage is another yellow-toned planting. Here, the little golden-leaved *Disporum sessile* 'Golden Geisha' that I brought back from Japan is a color echo for *Convallaria majalis* 'Fernwood's Golden Slippers', *C. majalis* 'Gold Leaf', and 'Gold Heart' dicentra (now *Lamprocapnos*), among others. This dicentra was a sport, a little stem that turned yellow, of a regular bleeding heart found at Hadspen House in Somerset, England, and all 'Gold Heart' plants come from that. It's a pretty sophisticated combination, but I'm an equal-opportunity gardener—I also use sweet alyssum from a farm stand.

In April, change can be dramatic from the beginning of the month to the end. At Brandywine Cottage, we've already been celebrating spring for a couple of months. But by the end of April, as temperatures accelerate, the season really takes off—if it's a normal year. Dogwoods bloom along with the tulips, trees begin to leaf out, and winter is just a memory. We continue the process of bringing plants out of the barn or the house, where the more cold-susceptible varieties have been vacationing. And in April my birds are back. They flash around the woodland, their songs fill the air, and for a moment, all is right with the world. These are the experiences that make me want to garden more.

Tulips: jewels in the garden

FROM OTTOMAN EMPERORS to gardeners today, tulips have been treasured as the perfect heralds of high spring. Color is what I think of when I think of tulips. The stunning color possibilities seem almost unlimited; few other plant groups offer as many variants. I often refer to tulips as one of my plant indulgences. (Yes, dear reader, I have more than a few.) Looking back, I can see that the fascination began early. As a child, I was in charge of all plant things outdoors. These were mostly fun things, but I earned a weekly allowance for my efforts. I remember one year wheedling my parents into giving me an advance on my allowance because I wanted to buy tulip bulbs. And I didn't want just a couple, but a few each of every tulip in the bulb catalog. Amazingly, they let me. It added up to several hundred bulbs—enough to line the front walk and driveway. I planted them in a single row, little sentinels all along that lengthy expanse. Come spring, it was a riot of bright color. People would come by and say, "Oh, Mrs. Culp, how colorful your garden is." I looked at it, and realized they were right—it was indeed very colorful. Even at that young age, I recognized that it was perhaps too much. My mother, bless her, loved it because I did it. But never again did I do anything like that. I learned quickly to plant larger drifts of one color and not to plant anything in soldierly rows.

I still enjoy browsing the bulb catalogs, however. To get all the tulip colors I crave, I make sure I fill out the order form early—in spring, while the colors I want more of are still fresh in my mind. Then I wait until the end of the bulb-selling season for closeout sales. But whether they are bargain bulbs or full-price must-haves, the tulips I acquire are divided into four basic categories, according to how I'll use them: border tulips (usually lily-flowering, Darwin, and viridiflora), cutting garden (anything goes), gravel garden (species and miniatures), and ruin garden (Rembrandts or broken tulips, and more species). All these bulbs will be planted in naturalistic drifts, except for those in the cutting bed.

above

There are certain tulips that I use just in my borders, including *Tulipa* 'Queen of Night' and *T.* 'White Triumphator'. This is a signature moment: white and black tulips with white-flowering dogwoods and a white picket fence, tying the garden to the white cottage.

above right

Tulipa 'Spring Green' with 'Gold Heart' dicentra.

Border tulips. My theme for the main beds is black and white—black Darwin ('Queen of Night') and white lily-flowering ('White Triumphator'). I plant 1,000 to 1,500. Simple yet dramatic, and maybe the one time of the year when my garden looks very color-controlled. Perhaps I'm channeling Chanel! Some years I drift another color in, a little magenta perhaps, just to break it up. But it is always predominantly black and white. I put new bulbs in among the old bulbs every year because I like the effect. The second-year bulbs are often smaller in flower size, which gives the appearance of self-sowing. I plant the tulips in the middle to back of the border, which allows the foliage to die back unseen, hidden by the upcoming perennial foliage. I use viridiflora tulips in the peripheral borders—the jewel box and the rose pillar, for example—and 'Spring Green' is my go-to first choice. It is lovely underneath white dogwood, and it ties in nicely with the white lily-flowering tulips in the main borders.

Tulips in the cutting garden, a
luxury that everyone should have,
if they have the space.

Cutting garden. I usually start by choosing colors that I would like to see used together. If you don't know where to begin, look around your house for colors that you use inside (we tend to repeat colors that we like on a fairly frequent basis), and use those as a guide; match your tulips to a color in your carpets or curtains, perhaps. I put my parrot, fringe, and other unusual tulips here as well; such divas stand out too much in the open garden and need a stage of their own. I have this feeling about many double and overdone flowers—they are beautiful but don't play well with others. They are lovely for arrangements, however, and parrot tulips have often been featured in Dutch paintings. The cutting garden provides plenty of early, mid-, and late-flowering tulips for arrangements for the house and for displays at our weekly Quaker Meeting.

Gravel garden. The tulips are at their most perennial here, as the gravel garden closely resembles their native habitat in the mountains of Central Asia. There the soil is lean and well drained, as it is in my gravel garden/driveway. Cars were long ago banished from the gravel garden space, which was once a parking area at the end of the drive. As a bonus, the squirrels and chipmunks don't like to dig in the gravel, so they leave the bulbs alone. I think the stones hurt their paws. Here I use species and dwarf-flowering forms, like *Tulipa bakeri* 'Lilac Wonder'.

Ruin garden. The Rembrandts or broken tulips are confined to the ruin garden, created within the crumbling stone walls of an old stable that collapsed many years ago. As it is walled on three sides, visually segregated from the rest of the garden, I can make my planting as whimsical as I wish, a veritable kaleidoscope of heights and textures and colors. The broken tulips certainly add to the show. It was their ability to "break" in color that fed the 17th-century Tulip Mania in the Netherlands: instead of being a solid color, their flowers may be feathered or flamed in an array of patterns as individual as snowflakes—an effect caused by a virus, although speculators didn't know that at the time. Fortunes were spent on individual bulbs, until the market dramatically collapsed. At the end of the 19th century, Dutch growers quit growing the broken tulips because the virus could ruin their vast fields of pure-colored ones. I mourn their loss. I can't help it—broken tulips are truly beautiful things; they remind me of paintings by the Dutch Masters. I seek out specialty nurseries that still offer them, and I have some that are older than my 18th-century house. Here I also use *Tulipa acuminata* (fire flame tulip). The form of its flower, refined and exquisite, is often depicted on tiles in the Middle East. It and all species tulips remind me of the ancient nature of tulips in the garden.

As for planting tips, basically, it's pointy side up. You plant tulips two to three times the depth of the bulb, but much shallower if you garden on clay soils. Cut the flower back after it ceases to close at night.

above

Rembrandt tulips. The virus does not bother me, and when I look at them I understand why Tulip Mania happened. From left: 'Insulinde' (1914); 'Absalon' (1780); 'Zomershoon' (1620).

This allows the bulb to store more nutrients instead of putting its energy into seed production, increasing the chances you'll keep your tulips for another year. If you cannot cut the flower off, at least cut off the old stems when the bulb has done flowering completely. It simply looks better.

Don't expect tulips to come back forever. Enjoy them with your whole heart, even if it is just for one season. And if you live in deer country, realize that tulips are deer food. I quite expect that one day they will find my tulips and eat them all. For the last 25 years, I have maintained a schedule of spraying with deer-repellent—one of those foul-smelling mixtures that deer supposedly hate. Originally I did this once a month, then it was every two weeks, and finally twice a week. It has worked, up until now. But last summer, the deer found my garden and ate all the hosta and the Solomon's seal. Sometime soon, I'm sure, they will dine on my tulips. What to do? I'm considering my options, which range from a simple strand of electrical wire to scare them off, to deer fencing. It's a choice that is hard to make.

Wildlife begins at home

I'VE ALWAYS HAD A STRONG CONNECTION to the natural world and a fascination with living things. I owe a huge thank-you to my parents for fostering this interest, although often it was not easy on them. Escaped hamsters chewed holes in the rugs, flying squirrels ran loose through the house, aquariums leaked. I once tried to incubate pigeon eggs in the oven; my mother later found them, rotten. (I asked for and received a two-egg incubator that Christmas.) My bedroom was full of plants, birds, and jars of bugs. My mother used to say she was afraid to put her hands in my pockets, for fear of what she might find. You could tell there was a young naturalist in the house, but my parents' simple rule was that if I took care of it, I could keep it. That golden rule has guided me my entire life: "You have to take care of it, David."

My grandparents too encouraged my core value of stewardship; on their farm, I had a pony, a calf, piglets, chickens, the natural world around me, and the mountains beyond. They taught me the rhythms of the earth. There is now a name for all this: ecological gardening. It means harmonizing with nature, welcoming and living with species other than our own, and re-establishing natural cycles in our gardens.

From the moment I saw it, I was drawn to the history of this property, the simple lines of the house, and the varied topography of the land. There was room for my two bulldogs to amble about; I could garden here in an ecological way, for wildlife and for us. Right away, I decided to leave the snag trees up in the woodland, as they often become homes for birds; this was their habitat as well. Fallen leaves were left to decompose on the hill-side, to feed the soil and to provide a home for insects, which in turn feed the birds and other creatures like lizards and snakes. Pollinators are vital to gardens, so there would be no spraying of herbicides or pesticides, ever. I can live with a chewed leaf or two, but I cannot live without my dogs, my birds, and other wildlife. I wanted to create a space where we all could live.

The house appealed to me because there is no wasted space; I'd rather have a smaller house and a larger garden. I encourage our bull-dogs to stay out of the borders, and they are good about that—most of the time. When they do decide to take a run, it has the same effect as rolling a bowling ball through the borders. Bulldogs are good (our family has kept them since I was in high school), but, like humans, perfect only in being imperfect. I remember one day I found Rose (our beloved red bulldog, now long departed) sunning herself in a border, in the middle of a patch of pink dianthus. I caught my breath—but quickly decided that I would do the same thing if I could. Oh, Rose! We have three bulldogs now, a

multi-generational family—furry, friendly lives that fit seamlessly into the fabric of our own. When I met Michael, I discovered that he had never had an inside dog of his own. The first thing I gave him was a bulldog named Katy. It was the perfect gift. He loves the dogs. This is what my parents did for me—they gave me something I could nurture.

On the farm, my grandparents gave me bantams of my own, and I keep bantams to this day, Old English bantams that are about the size of a crow. They don't do much damage, as they can walk under most plants. They eat all kinds of insects, so you could consider them my IPM (Integrated Pest Management) team, perhaps. Or, you could think of them as moveable art as they dart around the garden. They add a certain aesthetic, but this is a bantam-chicken garden, not a peacock garden. A little more understated. We get eggs, and sometimes baby chicks. I like the sounds of the crowing rooster, and the hens happily singing. I let the bantams out only when I am in the garden to keep an eye on them, as we have to watch for hawks or owls, which might see our chickens as dinner. Both have nested in the garden in different years. The great horned owls were a particular favorite, their chorus of haunting hoots never ceasing to mesmerize and thrill me, a sound so primal yet reassuring. A pair in the tree right behind the house gave us two chicks to watch, and they were very entertaining. We named them Owlbert and Owlvin.

My barometer for "doing things right" in creating a habitat is how well my plants, the wild birds, and the insects thrive and interact in the garden. Each is dependent on another. For the last couple of years, I have been keeping bees at the cottage. Seriously keeping them, that is, for I tried to keep them in my room as a child. I had read that hives can create a queen of their own, so in my childlike way, I thought I could get them to do this. I cannot tell you how many times I was stung as I was collecting bees. I had gallon jugs with holes in the lids sitting around, with twigs and flowers to give them nectar. I guess I didn't read the fine print—that you need a hive. My parents allowed me to keep a menagerie, but they drew the line at having a hive in the house. But I never gave up the idea. I just had to wait a few decades.

More than ever, with habitat loss and die-off, bees need our help, and we need them, if we are to survive. So I put an empty hive into our

left
What cultivar is it? Even the bantams get in on the act.

new meadow, and within a month a wild swarm had moved in. It felt like Mother Nature giving me her seal of approval. I'm tending the bees myself, under the guidance of Jeff Bryer, of Bryer Apiary. Do you think I know anything about bees? No, I don't, but I'm learning. It's a little daunting, but I like that challenge. And tasting the first raw honey from my own hive was a revelation, like sipping the finest wine after drinking the dregs. It was as if my garden were distilled in that honey. I'll never be able to eat store-bought honey again!

Most of us try to incorporate what we love and what we find beautiful into our lives. That's why it's good to travel, to walk in the woods, to go to museums—whatever reinforces our sense of what is beautiful, or is a source of inspiration. I love music and still find inspiration in a night at the symphony, but I can be equally happy with the music of a wood thrush. And that musical sensibility carries indoors. My Grandmother Culp kept a canary and as long as I can remember my parents had a canary in the house. I've always had one at Brandywine Cottage, and even before. Their songs brighten every day, even the most dreary, by bringing the outside in. I enjoy their presence, too—that little flash of yellow that I catch out of the corner of my eye, or the cheerful chirping that sounds like, *Hello, hello.*

A cottage property is not for everyone, but for me this is not just a house but my home, where I try hard to maintain a balance among visual impact, emotional experience, and biodiversity. I made the garden; the garden made me. Who knows if I can make a difference in the larger garden of our world, or if it is too late; but I do think that we must always try to do our best in our own space.

opposite
Yours Truly, checking his bees. A large part of the garden is a pollinator garden.

SAUTÉED FIDDLEHEAD FERNS

INGREDIENTS

1 lb freshly picked organic fiddleheads

1 tbsp sea salt; more salt to taste

2 tsp butter or olive oil

1 clove garlic (or small shallot, if you prefer)

1 lemon

Fiddleheads (so-called because they look like the scrolled end of a violin) are the tender, tightly coiled tips of new fronds on ostrich ferns (Matteuccia struthiopteris). Sautéed fresh fiddleheads have a delicate flavor, almost a sweetness, that you can only have in spring. We're talking a window of just a few weeks, because in a warm spell the ferns will grow about a foot. Fiddlehead ferns have been part of traditional diets for centuries in many countries around the world. We have them all along the drive. If you don't have ostrich ferns in your own garden, you can often find them in spring at farmers' markets.

METHOD

Put 2 quarts of water into a large pot and bring it to a boil. Meanwhile, check the fiddleheads carefully and remove any brown or suspect bits, then rinse them thoroughly in cool water. Blanch the cleaned fiddleheads by adding them and the sea salt to the boiling water. Boil for a minute. Drain and rinse the fiddleheads in cold water to cool, then spread them on paper towels and pat dry. Blanching should remove any bitter taste from the fiddleheads.

Peel the garlic (or shallot) and slice it thinly. Don't chop or mince it—you want it to enhance the delicate grassy flavor of the fiddleheads, not overwhelm it.

Heat the butter or oil in a large frying pan and add the blanched fiddleheads. Sauté until they start to brown on the edges—about 5 minutes. Add the garlic or shallot slices and continue sautéing until the garlic just starts to color. Salt to taste. Serve immediately with a lemon wedge on the side.

Note: Do not undercook the fiddleheads; online reports mention diners becoming ill after eating fiddleheads. Thorough cooking for safety is recommended. It could be that any food poisoning is the result of contaminants on wild-collected ferns; knowing the organic provenance of your fiddleheads is an advantage.

opposite
Sautéed fiddlehead ferns are a spring delicacy.

FUNNY CAKE

INGREDIENTS

Top portion

2 cups sugar

½ cup shortening (Crisco)

2 eggs

1¼ cups milk

¾ tsp vanilla

2 cups flour

2 tsp baking powder

¼ cup pecan pieces

Lower portion

1 cup sugar

½ cup cocoa powder

1 cup hot water

2 8-inch pie crusts

It's called Funny Cake because it is not really a cake, and not really a pie. It's funny like that. The bottom is a pie crust filled with a chocolatey mixture, and the top is a white cake with nuts on top. This is a specialty of eastern Pennsylvania Mennonites, including those from Bucks, Montgomery, Chester, Lehigh, and Berks counties.

It is also known as a breakfast cake, because it was eaten by farmers before they went out in the very early morning to milk the cows—before breakfast. It would really give them a needed energy boost. This cake includes secret ingredients that contribute to the success of the garden—chocolate and caffeine. Many a morning I've gone out into the garden after eating a piece of Funny Cake with my coffee, and before I realize it, several hours have passed.

Funny Cake, because it's also a pie, rates as one of my "Five Pies of Heaven"—apple, funny cake, ground cherry, Grandmother Rittenhouse's coconut cream, and grape strip pies. These are my favorites, but I'm always open to trying new contestants.

METHOD

Preheat oven to 350 degrees Fahrenheit.

Using a stand or hand mixer, cream sugar and shortening together. Add the eggs, then add the milk and vanilla. In a bowl, mix flour and baking powder with a fork, and gradually incorporate this into the batter. Pour the batter into the pie crusts. In another bowl, mix sugar, cocoa, and hot water together until blended and sugar dissolved, and pour over the pie batter. Sprinkle pecan pieces over the top. Bake for 50 minutes.

opposite
Funny Cake, also known as breakfast cake, is for me an "anytime cake."

MAY

DURING MAY THE GARDEN comes into full flush. It seems like yesterday the ground was nearly bare—we were looking at snowdrops and hoping for other things to come. Life has suddenly happened, and plants and weeds are growing fast. The late tulips are still in bloom, flaunting their colors. The garden is full of fresh green leaves.

As ours is a cottage garden, we grow many traditional cottage plants—foxgloves (*Digitalis*), phlox, polygonatums, and especially peonies. After the initial cost, these require little attention. Herbaceous peonies don't have to be lifted or divided every year, and the foliage can be attractive for most of the growing season. The species peonies come into bloom first, lovely with their single flowers. Among these are *Paeonia mollis*, *P. obovata*, and *P. mlokosewitschii* ("Molly-the-witch"). There are also species look-alikes, such as 'Early Scout', a fern-leaf hybrid. I tend to like the single peonies as much as, if not more than, the doubles, which are like divining rods for mud. When it rains, the showy doubles tend to become water-laden and, if not staked, soon bend to the ground, and the big flowers rot. The double flowers are beautiful, however. Like double hellebores, they add depth to the collection—and to arrangements. So I stake them, or put hoops around the plants well before they come into flower. That way their foliage hides the supports and they don't look so corseted. Every year I seem to find room for just one more peony to tuck in between shrubs or at the edge of the wild garden, and I've even created a cutting bed for them. I don't think there is any peony I could grow tired of, doubles or singles. Like hellebores, peonies don't like to be planted too deeply, and they don't like too moist a site. They like it on the dry side. If by chance they get powdery mildew or some other fungal problem in the late summer, I cut them to the ground and throw the old foliage away (never compost diseased foliage).

Think a little more carefully about where you will site cultivated tree peonies (*Paeonia suffruticosa*), because once you plant them you need

Pathways move you through the garden, both literally and visually. Here, note the positive and negative spaces, the borders positive and ebullient against the straight lines and tightly clipped pathways that surround them. The east wall of the house was left unplanted to create negative space to contrast with the effusive borders.

opposite
Peonies are a classic May flower, and that makes for classic arrangements. I always think of peonies as being in bloom around Memorial Day. I like them so much that as you can see I grow many different kinds.

above
Anemone flower form is one of the peony flower types I enjoy. I like the singles, especially for garden use— and doubles for cutting, since they flop over in the garden, anyway.

above right
Intersectional peonies, a cross between tree peonies and herbaceous peonies, prolong the peony season. They are the last ones to bloom for me in the garden.

to leave them alone. Each year they will get better and better. I don't recommend tree peonies as cut flowers. The only time I come at them with a pair of shears is to prune out any dieback that may have happened in a harsh winter. Tree peonies tolerate a little more shade, which is especially beneficial when we have high temperature spikes, because the blooms don't shatter so fast. In some Asian countries, gardeners help the blooms last longer by putting special parasols over the plants to protect them from the midday sun. If the parasols were available here, I'd probably do that myself. The blooms are so beautiful!

Along with peonies, another plant that belongs in any cottage garden, old or new, is bleeding heart. There are many forms, including *Dicentra eximia* (fringed bleeding heart), *D. formosa* (Pacific bleeding heart), and *D. peregrina*, an alpine species native to Japan and Siberia. However, *Lamprocapnos spectabilis* is the most popular bleeding heart. I grow the straight species, the white form, and 'Gold Heart', whose golden foliage adds a punch of color to my plantings. I use chartreuse or yellow tones throughout the garden to give a sense of unity, and because it brightens up my somewhat low-lying garden. I just love playing with color. Twenty years ago, I did not use yellow so much, but my taste has changed. I find myself using it more, and pairing it with colors I might not have considered in the past. Our color sense evolves—and let's face it, as I write this, I realize I will probably have changed my mind again by this time next year.

There is something about blue. The color goes with pastels and also with hot color combinations. I use this appealing color everywhere in the garden. I love the time of the year that forget-me-nots are in flower—their color unites the plantings with a carpet of blue. Some people complain that *Myosotis sylvatica* sows around too much, but I count on it! I can always pull out unwanted plants, or transplant them to other areas of the garden. For me, the hardest part of growing forget-me-nots is letting them go to seed, and that you must do if you want them to come back the following year. I leave them alone until they start to look disreputable; you have to let them get to that stage to ensure next year's display. After I cut them back, I fill the holes with summer-flowering annuals. Forget-me-nots like sun to part sun and well-drained soils (*M. scorpioides* will take moist soils), and they are very easy to grow once established—always reliable, not fussy.

Lily of the valley (*Convallaria majalis*) is the birth flower for the month of May. I've traded with like-minded collectors for many of the nine selections I grow: a yellow-leaf form, 'Hardwick Hall' (yellow-edged leaves), 'Variegata', pink flowering, white flowering, a form from Japan with splashed foliage, 'Crème de la Mint' (similar to 'Hardwick Hall'), a double-flowered form, and a pink-flowered clump-forming one from Germany. They are charming in the garden and in bouquets, and they perfume the air with their fragrance. They will cover space rapidly, which may be a problem in smaller gardens.

above
I grow nine different lilies of the valley in my garden, all selections of *Convallaria majalis*. From right: 'Variegata'; var. *rosea*; 'Fernwood's Golden Slippers'; 'Flore Pleno'; 'Crème de la Mint'; and a splashed form with an untranslatable name that I brought back from Japan.

Of course, one can always dig them up and plant them elsewhere, or give them to a friend. They may be shy to flower the following year, but I wouldn't be without them. They like part shade, average to dry soils, and are long-lived.

Alliums, one of the best parts of the May garden, never cease to bring smiles to the faces of my garden guests, and me. The borders are filled with *Allium schoenoprasum* and purple *A.* 'Globemaster'. They are so whimsical, like purple bubbles floating above the border. They serve as a focal point for all the green in the garden, uniting it even while providing a structural contrast to all the vertical shapes, such as foxgloves,

above
From left: *Allium schoenoprasum*; *A. cristophii*; *Nectaroscordum siculum* (Sicilian ornamental onion).

iris foliage, rose tuteurs, the picket fence. If you want your garden to have more drama, you'll have contrasting verticals and horizontals in the garden. That point where planes intersect—the vertical and the horizontal—is where the tension and the drama lie. The more of these you create, the more dramatic your garden will be. Structure speaks about emotion; color speaks about mood. First create the structure, then overlay it with color. The flowers of *A. karataviense* are a lovely pale lavender, but it's the foliage I like. It has the widest leaves of any allium I know, and the flowers sit atop these beautiful leaves. Alliums have been cultivated for millennia; we grow them in our vegetable gardens—onions, garlic, chives, scallions, shallots—and many of the non-edible species appear in the rock garden, perennial borders, and meadow. Of the ornamental alliums, I recommend *A. cernuum* (nodding onion), which has purple flowers that bloom in summer, for the rock garden; *A. cristophii* (star of Persia), which has football-size flowers, for the border; *A. rosenbachianum* (showy Persian onion), which is easy to grow; and *A. hollandicum* 'Purple Sensation', which is a little darker shade of purple. It's worth noting that most onions come from drier habitats.

Cypripediums are lovely, but 20 years ago, I would not have included them in a lecture or an article. I was concerned about these hardy orchids being collected in the wild, but with advances in tissue culture, my view has changed. *Cypripedium kentuckiense* and *C. parviflorum* var. *pubescens* were the first nursery-propagated species that would grow for me. After years of breeding and trialing orchids, I would sum up their culture by saying that good drainage and soils rich in humus or leaf mold are key. The fact that they need more sun than I had expected was a surprise; in nature, you usually will find them at the edge of woods. But the real game changers in recent years are the complex hybrids, which provide many new forms and colors for the garden, with the added bonus of being willing to live. They look great combined with woodland ephemerals—trilliums, disporums, polygonatums, ferns, bleeding hearts. Cypripediums just kick your combinations up a notch or two. It's really wonderful to walk down the garden path with terrestrial orchids blooming on either side. It's proof, I think, that there is a heaven.

This month isn't only about what's blooming in the garden. It's a busy time in the vegetable garden, too. Cool-season crops—lettuces, radishes, early peas, sorrel, rhubarb, watercress, strawberries—are already being harvested, and Michael has gathered baby carrots from the pots where he is growing them in light soil to encourage larger, straighter roots. By May, we are firmly past our last frost date, so we can start planting tomatoes and other cold-sensitive vegetables. If you put these out too early, a late frost or even very cool weather can set your plants back.

In late spring, indoor arrangements benefit not only from armfuls of flowers from the cutting garden but from branches of flowering shrubs as well. Viburnums are a signature Delaware Valley plant. Like dogwood, redbud, or quince branches, viburnum branches evoke a drive through the mid-Atlantic countryside on a sunny day. I see the wild viburnums, and then in the garden I will use more cultivated versions. And viburnums are just so elegant-looking. The strength of simple things, and the beauty of simplicity—to me, it speaks volumes. I like arrangements like that. Many times less is more.

Nature contained: delights of a moveable garden

WE LOVE AND RELY ON CONTAINERS here at Brandywine Cottage. At last tally, we counted about 400 of them, and we celebrate every one. They bring delight to gardening year-round, both outside and in. They allow you to create looks that you may not be able to replicate in the larger, in-ground garden, such as different color combinations, or groupings of plants that you wouldn't normally grow together. You can highlight collections of plants, such as hepaticas or begonias or succulents. You can create edible containers or herbal containers. You can group annuals and perennials and woody plants. And you can use them as moveable accents throughout the garden.

I think people traditionally thought of containers as entry accents to a house or property. Or maybe as a tender-plant centerpiece on a table, in the garden or indoors. But there is a container to suit almost any space in the garden. If a bare spot develops in a border, you can fill it with a potted plant, or use a container as a placeholder until you decide what to plant there. A container may prove easier to use than planting in the ground in tough areas, such as under trees or in shade. By managing the type of soil and the amount of water, you can provide cultural conditions in containers that may not be available elsewhere in the garden, such as well-drained soil in troughs for succulents, or moisture-retentive soil for bog gardens. Not every pot has to be planted. Some can be used as accents in their own right—my collection of Japanese cachepots, displayed on a high shelf in the basement, for example.

Many gardeners don't venture beyond tender plants or houseplants for use in containers, and that's fine. We like to mix them up. Although

above
The ruin garden houses a large proportion of our container collection.

opposite
Everything is fair game in a container. Here, lettuce is used as an underplanting.

borderline-hardy collections of plants such as hepaticas and arums are perfect for containers because you can move them in when the weather gets too cold, almost anything is suitable for a container. We use annuals, vegetables, herbs—whatever suits our needs; and we probably use as many perennials and woodies as annuals in our containers. Maybe even more. They live as container plants until we want a change or they outgrow the pot, and then we plant them in the open garden. I really like that they do double duty. And we often theme these containers, so that the display highlights a collection; our hepaticas may be grouped atop the covered well at the front of the cottage, for instance.

We change our entry containers often. These large pots might have semi-permanent anchor plants, such as a phormium or a grass or a big coleus, but we rotate smaller plants in and out according to the season or my whim. It creates an ever-changing tableau—the last thing you want is a static look.

I keep a supply of unplanted pots in the shed, ready to use, so I don't have to go searching when I want to make a new container planting. I mostly use terracotta—it brings a sense of unity to the garden—but also stone troughs or hypertufa. We like containers that look natural. I think the container should fit the character of the garden: if you have a contemporary garden, you should have contemporary containers.

Years ago, British garden designer Penelope Hobhouse shared this advice about containers: "Whenever you can afford it, buy two the same. That way, you can use them as pairs, or if one breaks, you have a replacement." Good, sound advice, and having two identical pots at different places in the garden also lends a certain unity, a familiarity of space. Of course, buying two is sometimes a hard pill to swallow, considering the price of some of the pots!

Some containers, such as those planted with woodies and perennials, are left out year-round. These are usually larger pots, chosen to give insulation to the plants' roots. But when it's time to bring the rest in for the winter—well, let's just say that is a major time here at the cottage. We start weeks, maybe a month, before the anticipated first frost date. When temperatures dip below 50 degrees at night, we start bringing in the first wave of tender plants, such as begonias. The plants that will take a light frost (dip to freezing overnight), including agaves and phormiums, come in last. Michael cuts back and lifts the large tender plants, the colocasias and bananas, and stores them in the barn. Multiple plants fit into each big pot, and we put bricks under the pots to keep their roots in slightly warmer air. The dahlias are dug up, shaken off, and stored in plastic bulb crates. Everything is in by early November, with almost half the containers in the house and the rest in the barn.

Once the plants are safe from frost, we have to make decisions on where to place them all. The plants that will spend the next few months in the house are chosen for aesthetic reasons, or because they need more light or heat, or a more watchful eye in general. I use every one of the cottage's 20-inch-deep window sills as well as the stairwell garden (of which more later) and try to keep the plants in a state of suspension, with not much active growth. And of course during this time we cut down on watering because their needs are less.

Some people may think that having so many containers is a little over the top. Many gardeners are happy with just a few. But that's a choice each gardener has to make. Even if you have but one, celebrate it! We enjoy having several hundred to celebrate, and that celebration continues year-round.

above
Part of my clivia collection, tied together with terracotta. Clivias are a favorite indoor/outdoor plant for me—certainly one of my stars indoors during the winter months.

above right
A hypertufa bowl full of tender succulents.

CREAM *of* SORREL SOUP

INGREDIENTS

4 tbsp butter

½ cup chopped onion

4 tbsp flour

½ lb sorrel leaves, stripped
from the stems and packed

Salt and white pepper

4½ cups chicken broth

2 egg yolks

½ to 1 cup heavy cream

Nutmeg, freshly grated

Chopped chives for garnish

Sorrel is not included in many herb gardens in our country, which is a shame as it is so easy to grow. Once the soil has warmed in spring, plant seeds directly into the garden about 6 inches apart, barely beneath the soil surface, and keep the soil moderately moist until seeds germinate. Thin the plants when they are about 2 inches high. Sorrel is relatively carefree once established and can grow to about 2 feet tall. Leaves may be 3 to 6 inches in length. Start to harvest in late spring when the plants are about 6 inches tall. If you cut the outer leaves, the plant will continue to produce foliage, and you should be able to continue using the herb until fall.

Sorrel is widely used in French cuisine, especially in creamy soups and sauces. It has a lemony flavor, and younger leaves are slightly tangy. Larger leaves can be used like spinach, steamed or sautéed. This recipe was shared with us by Elise du Pont of Patterns, a renowned estate overlooking the Brandywine River; among its gardens is a large potager.

METHOD

In a heavy saucepan over low heat, sauté the onion in butter until transparent. Add the sorrel leaves, raise the heat to medium, and stir until the leaves wilt. Add flour and cook for 2 minutes, stirring constantly. Add the chicken broth, bring to a simmer, and cook for several minutes, then add salt and white pepper to taste. Allow to cool slightly.

In a bowl, beat the egg yolks with a small amount of the sorrel-and-chicken broth, and stir that into the mixture in the saucepan. Put the mixture through a blender, then strain into a bowl. Add cream and nutmeg to taste, then chill for at least 12 hours. (If you want a thinner soup, add more chicken broth or cream.) Serve in cold soup cups, with a garnish of chopped chives. This recipe yields about six 1-cup servings.

opposite
Cream of Sorrel Soup has a
delicate lemony flavor.

STRAWBERRY-RHUBARB UPSIDE-DOWN CAKE

Rhubarb is a cool-season crop that is usually ready to harvest starting in April, when the edible leaf stalks are deliciously crisp and tangy yet sweet. They are an ideal companion for strawberries in pies as well as preserves.

Harvest your rhubarb stalks when they are 10 to 15 inches long, but leave at least a third of the stalks on the plant, so it can recover. Grasp each stalk near the base and slowly pull and twist, or use garden shears. Make sure to cut off all leaves and discard them, as they are poisonous. The tender stalks can be frozen for later use, if desired.

This recipe from Michael's family takes him about 10 minutes to put together, and another 35 to 40 minutes to bake. I often request this dessert for my birthday.

INGREDIENTS

Rhubarb mixture

3 cups rhubarb, cut
   into ½-inch slices

½ cup strawberries,
   hulled and chopped

1 cup sugar

2 tbsp flour

Pinch of nutmeg

¼ cup butter, melted

Batter

1½ cups flour

¾ cup sugar

2 tsp baking powder

¼ tsp salt

Pinch of nutmeg

¼ cup butter, melted

⅔ cup milk

1 egg

METHOD

Rhubarb mixture: Sprinkle rhubarb and strawberry pieces in a greased 10-inch heavy skillet. Combine sugar, flour, and nutmeg, and sprinkle over rhubarb/strawberry combination. Drizzle with melted butter.

Batter: Combine flour, sugar, baking powder, salt, and nutmeg in a bowl. Add melted butter, milk, and egg. Beat until smooth.

Spread the batter over the rhubarb mixture, and bake at 350 degrees Fahrenheit for 35 minutes, or until done. Remove from oven, loosen edges immediately, and invert onto serving dish. Serve warm or cold, with whipped cream if desired. Makes 8 to 10 servings.

opposite
Strawberry-Rhubarb Upside-Down
Cake is a delicious conclusion to a
spring meal.

JUNE

JUNE SPEAKS TO ME of a certain fullness. The garden is growing happily, the birds are singing, the bees are buzzing. In June, the garden almost seems as though it could take care of itself. Everything seems to be moving forward—including the weeds. This is the time you discover you may have planted your plants too close together. Invariably, I have.

I've always felt that gardeners fall into two categories: those who don't like plants to touch, and as a result they tend to use a lot of mulch; and those who like the plants in close-knit communities, so they can't see any soil between them. I'm in the second group. In nature, plants have relationships. You just want them to play well with each other, so they all can thrive. I encourage them to do this by pulling some out or cutting them back if they start to feel too crowded. That's a constant in gardening—fine tuning, especially as the garden grows older. For the most part, the gardener's role is simply to referee.

June is the time when roses tumble over the walls and fences, like the apricot-flowered *Rosa* 'Ghislaine de Féligonde', spilling over the ruin garden wall. My garden, like the season, mirrors the roses in its opulence and effusiveness. A garden in June is easy to do, compared to those in February and March. I've always said that if a garden looks good in February, it will look good at any time of year. It helps if you start planning for June in the previous fall. I'm already planning for next year. The act of gardening is always a display of optimism. It's the nature of gardening itself—putting something in the ground with the expectation of seeing it mature in a year or two. And it's exciting. There's always one more combination to make, one more plant to acquire, one more thing to learn about the world in which we live.

Color looms large in June. The gray Scottish thistle (*Onopordum acanthium*), the emblem of Scotland, looks quite dramatic in combination with all my yellows. I like those thistles in the border, so I save the

above
I love the lush look that June imparts. Here we have an old rose, 'Ghislaine de Féligonde', tumbling into the ruin garden.

opposite
Vines, be they lonicera or clematis, are often intertwined with the climbing roses. Everything does double duty.

seed, which it is not readily available. It's one of the exuberant plants that have great texture, and you need texture in the garden. Some thistles are regarded as invasive weeds in certain parts of the country because they seed around so freely. Others are much loved. One, Miss Willmott's ghost (*Eryngium giganteum*), is named for English horticulturist Ellen Willmott of Warley Place, who so loved the plant she reportedly scattered its seed surreptitiously wherever she went. Even though she was no longer there, the story goes, you knew she had visited your garden.

I have quite a few climbing hydrangeas and relatives, including *Schizophragma hydrangeoides* var. *concolor* 'Moonlight' (Japanese hydrangea vine) and *Hydrangea petiolaris*, which enjoys a featured spot on the barn wall opposite our front door. Climbing hydrangeas don't go into the mortar like English ivy, so they're not destructive. Because of its prime spot, I started with a good-size plant that was already on a small trellis. It starts out slow and then goes gangbusters, flowering in June even in part shade, although it doesn't produce as much bloom on the shady side of the wall as on the sunnier side. All we do to this plant is trim it back in late June or early July to keep it from growing into the walkway and eaves. Any trimming must be done early, because it blooms on old wood—trim it much later and you risk cutting off the following year's flowers. *Hydrangea petiolaris* also has stunning yellow fall foliage and cinnamon-colored exfoliating bark in winter—truly a plant with four seasons of interest.

above

Vines knit things together and are wonderful vertical accents. From left: *Parthenocissus quinquefolia* 'Variegata'; *Lonicera sempervirens* f. *sulphurea* 'John Clayton'; *Humulus lupulus* 'Aureus' (golden hop).

opposite

In late spring a two-story wall of *Hydrangea petiolaris* flowers greets us when we walk out our front door.

When you walk down the steps leading to our front door, you see a sign that says "Bird Sanctuary." How can we encourage these colorful and fascinating creatures to frequent our gardens? We can start by offering them what they need. Water is perhaps most critical. From an ornate fountain to a simple birdbath, it's essential to have water for the birds. I also plant for them, establishing thickets, vines, and shrubs to provide protection and places for nests. Dead limbs and dead trees—as long as they are not dangerous or extremely unsightly—provide food for insects that the birds will then eat or feed to their young, as well as nesting places for woodpeckers and chickadees, among others. Shrubs or trees that have berries are particularly useful. Viburnums, dogwoods, crabapples, amelanchiers, the much-dreaded mulberry—all provide cover and food, as do numerous perennials, including seed-bearers like coneflowers and sunflowers. The sight of goldfinches gathering seeds from *Coreopsis tripteris* or sunflowers brings magical life to the garden; when I also see

a caterpillar on fennel, or a ladybug eating an aphid on the asclepias, I know everything is unfolding as it should.

I cannot imagine being in a garden with no natural sounds. It adds a dimension beyond the visual to our enjoyment of the garden. Over the years I've learned to pick out individual bird songs, and now I know my longtime friends and residents by song and by sight. When there is a hawk nearby, everything becomes very still, which is my warning to keep an eye on the bantams. They say that when the great Gertrude Jekyll was losing her eyesight, her sense of hearing became very acute; she could tell when she was near a stand of bamboo, for instance, from the sound the wind made moving the stalks. All the senses are heightened in the garden. The cottage garden is the local hub for lightning bugs (Pennsylvania's official state insect: *Photuris pennsylvanica*)—which is surprising because, unlike me, many of my neighbors use sprays. I hope we never lose the sense of wonder that allows us to be delighted by the sight of lightning bugs on a late spring night. With habitat loss affecting these and other pollinators in general (and bees in particular), we should all try to figure out ways to encourage them in our landscapes and gardens.

June may be filled with idyllic experiences, but there are also chores to do. Let's call this what it is: work. The way we garden at Brandywine Cottage, there is probably even more work than the norm, because we require more from the garden. I realize that. This month, we do a change-out, replacing the spring annuals with summer-blooming annuals, and pulling out any early-blooming plant that is looking tatty—including some of the biennials, such as the foxgloves. We do this not only in the borders but in the vegetable garden, where the lettuce and radishes come out to make way for peppers, eggplants, and anything else that likes the warmth. And it's not too late to plant seeds for summer crops or fall-blooming annuals. I like to get the bulk of my new planting done in

above
Black locust in flower. Some people consider this a trash tree; however, the bees and I beg to disagree. The flowers perfume the air in late May and June. It's a gorgeous tree.

opposite
I can see bird nests from four windows of the house. It's always a great joy to discover them.

Our terrace, off the south side of the house, reminds us to relax. With the addition of the cedar table, which recalls the cedar that was growing on the property, an outdoor space becomes our dining room.

June, before the weather gets too hot and the rains stop, as they often do in July and August.

The deadheading continues, too. I deadhead my roses, especially the ones that like to repeat, unless it's a rose that develops attractive hips, such as the rugosas and some shrub roses. This is also when we begin work on the summer cutting garden, pulling out the tulips and replacing them with dahlias, which we've collected for years; every year we buy four or five new ones, always cut-and-come-again varieties. So much lush growth at this season makes it easy to bring armloads of outdoor beauty in.

The long list of chores may seem daunting sometimes, but try to relax and take time to enjoy the delights of your June garden. The trick is to look at what you have accomplished, not what you have yet to do. Every time I catch myself thinking about what I still have to do, I try to appreciate what is already done—or, as Joanna Reed used to call it, "backing into your work." Remember, we do this because we love it.

Continuing the conversation, inside and out

WE LOVE FINDING WAYS to bring the outdoors inside, and one of the easiest ways to do this is by making flower arrangements. For us, they are as vital to our way of living as food—food for the body, plants for the soul.

The way we garden provides a wealth of material for creativity. The perennial borders, the cutting beds, the woodland, and the woodland's edge offer plenty of opportunities to glean bits and pieces for our arrangements, and evening walks and roadside weeds add to the natural mix. But we have no qualms about adding a few touches from the grocery store or flower shop when necessary. When we prune the borders, we make arrangements out of those clippings, too. Just as in the garden, everything is fair game: grasses, branches, leaves, weeds, buds, berries, fruits, ferns—and flowers, of course. Whatever catches our eye may become part of an ephemeral work of art.

We've had a cutting garden for years now, in a fairly large work area screened off from the garden proper by a hedge of *Cryptomeria japonica* (Japanese cedar). Initially, we used the space as an overflow area for vegetables, and sometimes dahlias. It still accommodates our snowdrop and hellebore stock beds, and the mother beds where I bulk up one-of-a-kind varieties. A cutting garden allows you to bring the outside in without having any visual impact on the rest of the garden. It also encourages

opposite
A simple vase of feverfew flowers looks fresh indoors on a table or mantel.

114 * LATE SPRING

a collector to indulge a love of particular plants, or to grow them in colors that may not fit with the design of the garden.

We always have something blooming in our garden, and Michael and I love to share this bounty with our Quaker Meeting as an offering, a floral ministry of sorts. Plants are what we are given, and arrangements are what we can give back each week. As it happens, one member of our Meeting, Enid Brown, had done this for 33 years, until she died shortly before I became a member. I found this out the first time I put an arrangement in the window, about a decade ago; another member asked, "Did Enid send you?" I'm not sure I'll make it for 33 years, but our arrangements, like Enid's, are an offering of love.

Michael does a lot of the floral arrangements and has a natural flair for it. We often do what I call mono-plant arrangements, or we adopt a varied floral style, but our hope is always that the arrangements look fresh and not overly stylized. A loose, informal, country style suits us. Some of my personal favorites include what others may think of as weeds, putting them all together to make a lovely picture.

I try to persuade my family to bring nature indoors, too. I gave each of my nieces a vase as a thank-you gift, and told them it was my hope that they would always have fresh flowers in the house. If they see the vase sitting empty, I hope they will remember to fill it, if only with a bouquet from the grocery store. I tell them flowers are just as important as the milk on the shopping list. Of course I say it is even better to take a walk and bring something you like inside, whether it's a flowering branch or a bit of moss. Use your imagination. And I assure them of this, too: "It pleases me to think that you are appreciating nature, and I will always be with you as you do this." My secret hope is that they will be inspired and will want to do more with plants outside. If not, I am content with the fact that they are enjoying flowers inside. That is enough. But the whole family now forces paperwhites at the holidays, so I have had some effect.

Still-life arrangements of fruit, flowers, vegetables, and other inanimate objects have figured in Western art for hundreds of years. Like most

people, I thought of them as conceits for paintings, or for arrangements indoors. But then I thought, why not use them outdoors? I became convinced still-lifes could play an important role in the garden when I saw them used in gardens in Belgium and Holland. Voilà! Bring the indoors out. My taborets, for example, are influenced by images of miniature Shinto altars, as they are built of natural stone, without mortar and with perfect balance. Offerings to the Goddess Flora, perhaps.

Roses, loved by commoners and kings

MY FIRST ASSOCIATIONS with gardens all featured roses. And, like lots of people, I still think they are among the most beautiful flowers on earth. I have more than 50 roses in my garden, and I am constantly transported by their beauty of color and form. I love them best when they are somewhat unruly, spilling over walls and fences—nothing approaches the full, lush look they impart to the garden.

I have many old roses, and when they are blooming I am reminded of a conversation I once had with a rose expert in France. I remarked that the French use color differently from the English. She looked at me. "But of course we do!" I could see where that conversation was going; to my eye, the roses we were observing did clash somewhat, so I just added, "Well, they're brighter." Her response? "A rose is still a rose—what more do you want?" So I came back home and combined a purple and a yellow rose on the same tuteur—the rambler *Rosa* 'Veilchenblau' and the palest yellow antique climber *R.* 'Céline Forestier'. I do like the different trellises the French use, and the different ways they display their roses. I don't want my tuteurs to look structurally heavy. These roses are ramblers and climbers; I do trim them, but I'm of the school that a rose should look kind of wild. This may be why I am not as enthusiastic about hybrid teas; I think they are too studied.

Before planting a rose, you should assess the site, considering the habit of the rose you want to plant and the amount of space available.

Make sure the rose and the space are suited to each other. Personally, I like old shrub roses and climbing roses, which usually take up considerable space and add to the sense of effusiveness that I like.

Old roses are sometimes hard to find. I use mail-order sources for many of them, including Antique Rose Emporium and Roses of Yesterday & Today. Usually, any large metropolitan area will have at least one nursery that specializes in roses, such as Mostardi's near Philadelphia and Rohsler's outside New York. Many old shrub roses are available only in bare-root form. If you buy bare-root roses, you should plant them as soon as possible. If the roots look dried out, soak them in a bucket of water for an hour. Prepare a planting hole that is larger than the spread-out roots. Be sure the hole is well drained and amended with leaf mold, good topsoil, and perhaps even a little bone meal, if you have some. Do the best you can with the soil. I have found that roses respond to attention such as soil preparation and feeding with well-aged compost or the like. This is the one plant for which I do this.

Yes, I know the old roses are large plants, but you can see them from afar. I like the form and shape of their flowers, and I love the full-flowered, high petal count that many of the old roses have. But I also like the singles. My selections are also based on disease resistance, because I do not spray. There are so many roses to choose from, so if one is prone to disease, I remove it. Not spraying also influences the way I grow roses. If they seem susceptible to black spot, I underplant them with geranium, nepeta, euphorbia, and other perennials. Now, if they do get black spot, the unsightly foliage is hidden by their companions.

New roses do have qualities to admire. One thing I like about hardy, disease-resistant new roses like the Knock Out series is that when I drive around public areas and parks, it's nice to see roses again. These hardy roses are often planted in masses. I grow Double Knock Out roses in my garden. Somebody told me it was a color I wouldn't be able to use, so I had to prove them wrong. I put it in a far corner, and its color carries from a distance—although it grew taller than I anticipated.

And ah, the fragrance of roses, a fragrance equaled by few other flowers. Unfortunately, some of this special quality has been lost in many of the newer hybrids, but the breeders are working on it. Fragrance is

left
Roses are present in every border. Since I don't use pesticides, I underplant my roses with perennials, which befits the cottage style.

above
The exuberance and flower power
of Double Knock Out roses and
salvia, tamed somewhat in an
antique crock.

above right
Rosa 'Charles de Mills' is a fragrant
antique garden rose.

important. On a garden tour in France a while back, fellow rose aficionado Emily "Pemmy" Frick and I teamed up over a shared enjoyment of the varied fragrances. Pemmy knew of my passion for hellebores, but she also saw how much I loved roses. Almost every photo I have shows me with my nose pressed into a rose. "As much as you like roses," she urged me, "you should give up hellebores and grow roses instead." Of course, I stayed true to hellebores. But everyone really should take time to smell the roses—individually.

Iris, a rainbow of colors

IRISES HAVE LONG BEEN ASSOCIATED with human civilization, and their elegance has made them a symbol of royalty throughout history. As far back as 2000 BC, irises were depicted in Minoan murals on Crete, and they played a role in ancient Egyptian cultures as a sign of power. In Greek mythology, the goddess Iris was the personification of rainbows and a messenger of the Olympian gods. As part of her duties, she helped to fulfill humans' prayers. I need all the help I can get, so I plant lots of iris. It's fitting that the goddess of the rainbow wrapped her ribbons of color all around the world, as iris species can be found all around the world, too. The flower we recognize as an iris is a cross between a species from central Europe and a larger-flowered species from the Near East. Most species are native to the Mediterranean region.

With a little planning, you can have irises blooming in your garden from Mardi Gras to the Fourth of July, or even later. I start with the dwarf *Iris reticulata*, followed by *I. danfordiae*, *I. histrioides*, and *I. cristata*, as well as dwarf, intermediate, and tall varieties of *I. germanica* (German bearded iris). More examples of how you can extend the bloom time include *I. sibirica* (Siberian iris), *I. pseudacorus* (yellow flag), *I. ensata*

above
These are all Japanese iris (*Iris ensata*). They grow in average moisture-retentive soil and bloom in late June.

(Japanese iris), and Louisiana iris. Five different species make up what we know as the Louisiana group: *I. fulva*, *I. hexagona*, *I. brevicaulis*, *I. giganticaerulea*, and *I. nelsonii*. All are native to Louisiana and nearby regions, and although they sometimes grow in standing water, all are happy in ordinary garden soil with a pH of 6.5 or lower.

If you are bitten by the iris bug, as I am, you can find irises that bloom even later in the season, such as the reblooming cultivars of German bearded iris, including 'Immortality', 'Autumn Tryst', and 'Sugar Blues'. I tend to favor the tall German iris in the garden, especially the

heirloom cultivars. I prefer their elegance and simplicity of form, and antique cultivars are often more fragrant. Their form is more authentic for use in historic gardens, but their simplicity speaks to modern gardens as well. Heirloom irises are easy to grow, their tangles of tubers are easy to divide, and they are drought tolerant (they store water in their tubers). I grow the tall German bearded irises in borders and in accent drifts elsewhere. Dwarf German and intermediate German are perfect for the rock garden, and they also work well when planted toward the front of the borders or in accent areas.

These beautiful flowers were once colloquially called flags, reportedly from the Middle English word *flagge* for rush or reed. This old term reflects a certain sentimentality, which may be why irises were grown in or around cemeteries. Many are in bloom around Memorial Day, and the old varieties seem to thrive on neglect. Whatever you call them, irises planted with poppies and peonies will reward any gardener with a time-tested classic combination.

WATERCRESS TEA SANDWICHES

INGREDIENTS

8 oz cream cheese

1 cup fresh young watercress, chopped (remove any thick stems, as they may be fibrous and bitter)

White bread, thinly sliced

Sprigs of watercress for garnish

Few things are more quintessentially English than afternoon tea, where tea sandwiches play a starring role. But these delicate treats are also popular on this side of the Atlantic; I have enjoyed tea sandwiches almost all my life, at a variety of special family functions.

Originally, these little sandwiches were served—with hot tea, of course, and small iced (frosted) cakes—in mid to late afternoon; they were meant to stave off hunger until the evening meal was served, which in Victorian England was often not until 8 o'clock—so there was quite a gap between lunch and dinner. Back then, tea sandwiches had a light filling, no crusts, and were cut into rectangles or triangles that could be held in one hand and eaten in two bites; folklore suggests this was so Queen Victoria could both eat and converse.

Many popular garden vegetables make excellent tea sandwiches, from cucumbers and radishes to asparagus and tomatoes. This simple but delicious recipe is a classic pairing of cream cheese and watercress (Nasturtium officinale), which, although often thought of as simply a garnish, is one of the most nutritious foods you can eat, packed with nutrients, particularly vitamins K, C, and A, and historically grown for medicinal use. Watercress has a light, slightly peppery taste that works well in salads and sandwiches. It is readily available at farmers' markets and in produce departments; the easiest source of fresh and nutritious watercress, however, is your own garden.

These tasty sandwiches may be served for lunch or afternoon tea. But if you want to have your own Downton Abbey moment, set up your afternoon tea table under a shade tree in the garden.

METHOD

Thoroughly mix cream cheese with chopped watercress. Spread the mix on thin slices of white bread to make sandwiches. Trim all the crusts off the bread, and cut the sandwiches into rectangular fingers. If preferred, some of the finger sandwiches may be served open-face. Garnish with small whole leaves or sprigs of watercress.

opposite
Watercress Tea Sandwiches. In between all the chores, take time to enjoy your garden—perhaps with an afternoon tea. Sitting back and enjoying your garden is part of the experience, too.

GOOSEBERRY FOOL

INGREDIENTS

¾ lb gooseberries,
   topped and tailed

3 tbsp powdered sugar or
   finely granulated sugar

7 oz plain Greek yogurt

1 to 2 tbsp confectioner's
   sugar

1 tsp vanilla extract

1 cup heavy cream

Fresh mint leaves for garnish

Gooseberries have become more popular in recent years as American gardeners have embraced the idea of growing a variety of berries. These cool-weather berries can be eaten fresh or in desserts when ripe, or in jams and jellies using not-quite-ripe fruit.

Gooseberry Fool is a traditional dessert in England, possibly dating back to the 15th century; essentially, it's a mixture of whipped cream and pureed fruit. Fools can be made with almost any fresh fruit that can be pureed. Why "fool"? It's not clear; some sources say the name derives from the French word fouler, *meaning "to mash" or "press." This Gooseberry Fool is adapted from a British recipe.*

There are two major types of gooseberries—European (Ribes uva-crispa) and American (R. hirtellum). The native American gooseberry has smaller fruit and, some say, less flavor, but is easier to grow and more disease resistant. If you don't have gooseberries growing in your garden, look for them at farmers' markets in June or July. Failing that, substitute another seasonal fruit, such as strawberries, or use rhubarb. In fall, try it with fresh cranberries.

METHOD

Combine gooseberries, finely granulated sugar, and a spritz of water in a saucepan over medium heat. Stir the mixture as you bring it to a simmer, and continue stirring and cooking until the berries start to burst. Using a fork, mash the fruit to a pulp, then refrigerate the mixture until cold. Meanwhile, beat the yogurt, confectioner's sugar, and vanilla in a bowl until smooth. Gently whisk in the heavy cream until it thickens, then fold in chilled fruit mixture, leaving little swirls of berries visible. Spoon into shallow champagne glasses—or any pretty glass dessert dishes—and garnish with mint leaves to serve.

opposite
Gooseberry Fool is a traditional
English dessert. It may look special,
but it is easy to make.

SUMMER

opposite
Thalictrum rochebruneanum
'Lavender Mist'. I like the height of
meadow-rues—and the fact that
they are a see-through plant.

JULY

JULY USUALLY BRINGS SUNNY DAYS and vivid colors
in the garden. The bright colors are just what's needed to stand up to
the glaring sun overhead. It's no accident that the plants in hot tropical
regions are so vivid! Here, too, Mother Nature seems to be working with
a lot of yellows and other bright colors in meadows and roadsides at this
time of year. Some people like it, others don't. What's up with that? As
the gardeners, we are the artists, and it's our opportunity to make the
colors work.

I find it very easy to take up the summer yellow cue. Lilies, rudbeckias, daylilies all come in yellow, and they're all putting on a show this
month. My current impulse is to group yellows with apricots to soften
the tone. I also scatter them throughout the garden to help create a sense
of unity. Repetition, repetition, repetition—of color, of shape, or of a
particular genus—is an important part of the overall design. I'll repeat
a genus several times throughout the garden but use different species.
It helps knit the garden together and prevents it from looking choppy.
Although I want different experiences in different areas, I want the
entire space to work harmoniously. Otherwise, it's like walking through
a designer showcase, not a home garden. When you have different styles
in the garden, you have to have transitions from one area to another. And
when you can see several different areas at once—the borders, the jewel
box, the rose garden—you don't want it to be jarring. Gentle transitions.
In America, we tend to have fewer hedges and walls than they do in
England or Europe, where the garden areas are often visually separate.
Our gardens are more open. They may include a series of garden rooms,
but how you move through them becomes more important.

With yellow, I also use gray. The color gray has blue in it, and blue
with yellow is a natural combination, so why not gray as a companion
to yellow? Some of the plants I use that offer various shades of gray:
Artemisia 'Powis Castle', *A. schmidtiana* 'Silver Mound', *A. ludoviciana*

'Valerie Finnis', *Salvia argentea*, annual senecios, agaves, and yuccas. When your garden must face a hot, dry summer, you tend to think of Mediterranean or desert plants for inspiration. A lot of these plants are gray, or glaucous, because that reflects light, which helps to limit loss of moisture through evaporation. The same is true for the hairs on a lot of gray plants, such as *Stachys byzantina* (lamb's ear). Again, this is responding to the site. We don't have an irrigation system; we have chosen plants that work with the conditions we have.

We don't take our overwintered tropical plants out of the barn and into the garden until the roses are done. That would be mixing metaphors a little too much! When the weather gets hot, the phormiums, bananas, colocasias, cannas, and others give the garden a more exuberant, summery look. Michael loves them (he is the one who faithfully digs them up each fall), so for him this is a favorite time of year. When we get a lot of summer rain, as we sometimes do, the tropicals are particularly happy. In summer and fall, the borders get a bit blowsy, and we need

structural, architectural plants to hold everything together. These are big borders, 40 feet long and 15 feet wide. We need something big to provide scale and focus, or they will look a fuzzy mess. We can't rely on woodies for this, because our borders are 90 percent herbaceous plants, so this is where the big tropicals come in. They are quite at home with my tall perennials. Together, they take the garden to a whole new level.

Among the tall perennials I get a lot of enjoyment out of at this time of year are meadow-rues (*Thalictrum*). I love their scale, and the thalictrums provide me with big, cloud-like umbels of flowers, 6 to 8 feet tall. I grow yellow ones, such as *T. flavum*; purple ones, such as *T.* 'Splendide', *T.* 'Elin' (one of the tallest hybrids), and *T. aquilegiifolium* 'Purpureum'; and the white-flowered *T. aquilegiifolium* 'Album'. I use them not only in the back of the border but mid-border as well, because you can look through them. Like a lady looking through a veil, you can see what is behind them. I'm not one for the choirboy effect of stepped rows—tall ones in the back, short ones in the front! That is far too staged-looking for me.

left

As soon as rose season is over, we place our tropicals in the garden. They give an entirely different look to the garden, perfect for the hot summer sunshine.

above

Here among the perennials I place a huge agave affectionately known as "Big Bertha," which started out as a piece from Chanticleer. The affection wanes somewhat when we have to take her indoors.

above

Thalictrum flavum is about 7 feet tall. The yellow flowers are a nice cheery color. Most people think of meadow-rues as being lilac to lavender. I say have them all—yellow, blue, purple, white.

above right

A swallowtail butterfly enjoys the lilies as much as I do.

opposite

A carpenter bee on a phlox flower. We have many wild bees as well as my honeybees.

The lilies in the north border add to this towering scale, and *Phlox paniculata* makes its presence felt here as well. Earlier in the year, the tulips were at the back of this border; the new wave of plants not only camouflages their dying foliage but moves the color interest forward. None of the tall plants is staked. Most lilies are loved by butterflies, and when the phlox bloom, pollinator activity is magnified. The borders become pollinator heaven, especially when you add the late-summer lure of native eupatoriums (now sometimes called eutrochiums) like 'Gateway' and 'Bartered Bride'. Butterflies and bees love these tall Joe-Pye weeds, which, according to gardening lore, are named for Joe Pye, a Native American of the Algonquin tribe, who used concentrates derived from a species of the plant to cure fevers.

Astilbes are blooming in July. I prefer the ones that do double duty, that have interesting foliage as well as beautiful flowers. Case in point, *Astilbe* 'Delft Lace', which has purple foliage and pink flowers on red stems. Even if they are green, like *A*. 'Sprite', I like interesting foliage.

Pollinators also love *Asclepias curassavica*, a tropical milkweed that seeds itself around. Its two-tone effect separates it from our native milkweeds.

Hydrangea quercifolia Snowflake is a double-flowered form of oakleaf hydrangea. It is an accent plant.

'Sprite' is shorter and has heavily dissected leaves. Other favorites include *A. chinensis* varieties, because they are the most drought-tolerant. Here in the mid-Atlantic states, it's a bit hot for them to do well; they tend to do better in New England. I don't think big clumps look naturalistic. I use astilbes as accents rather than as major focal points.

Both phlox and beebalms are vigorous plants that have to be kept in check. I enjoy allowing all my plants to express themselves, but not to the extent of being bad neighbors and overrunning their companions. In July my biggest chore is pruning—pulling out weeds, cutting things back. I own pruning shears, and I'm not afraid to use them.

The hydrangeas continue their show in July and on into August. I have a couple dozen of these versatile shrubs dappled across the hillside, which can look remarkably lush in July, with just bits and pieces of *Hydrangea quercifolia* (oakleaf hydrangea) visible; it's amazing how that plant seeds around, but it shouldn't surprise me, as it is a native. On the hillside, creating a kind of tree-level design, is the white-flowered *H. arborescens* 'Annabelle', along with *Cornus controversa* 'Variegata', with its horizontal branches and leaves featuring bright creamy margins, and *Stewartia pseudocamellia*. I love them for their year-round interest and the way their white petals fall gracefully around.

This is also hosta time. I confess to having choice cultivars tucked throughout the shady areas of the garden. Unlike many hosta lovers, I use hostas not so much as a collection but as design elements and individuals. On the hillside, for example, I try to create the illusion that the hostas are naturalizing, spilling their offspring down along the steps toward the gravel garden. I do this by using large ones like *Hosta* 'Big Daddy' up the hill, giving way to the medium-size *H.* 'Blue Cadet' and then dwarf varieties. *Hosta sieboldiana* var. *elegans* plays the part of sentinel at the stairs. Any hosta with sieboldiana blood is a bit more tolerant of dry conditions, and the deep ribbing and thick texture make it harder for slugs to dig their holes in the leaves.

above
Container plants. From left: Jumbo alocasia with hakonechloa and farfugium; *Scadoxus multiflorus* subsp. *katherinae*, a summer-flowering AGM bulb; a garden-center begonia, simply because I like the shade of red.

Around the Fourth of July, we change many of our outdoor pots over to their summer look. One plant that threatens to burst out of its container is an enormous *Crinum americanum*, which has to be maneuvered indoors for the winter. A Southern native, it sits across the pathway from *Magnolia grandiflora* 'Edith Bogue', because in the wild they could have been natural companions. That magnolia and the nearby

above

Crinums are quintessential in many old gardens in the South, and I decided not to be without them. I grow them in containers. This is *Crinum americanum*, native to the southern United States.

M. virginiana create an arch—the tips of their branches are kissing. My theory is that plants are happier touching. They don't want to be surrounded by a yard of mulch.

By late July, the vegetable garden is producing a surfeit of food, including early tomatoes if we're lucky. Some years we get unwanted help with the surfeit in the form of groundhogs—and out come the Havahart traps. I prefer catch-and-release, but there are other ways to get around the problem: at one garden I was associated with we tried to buy the groundhogs off—we actually fed one peanut butter sandwiches to keep him away from the zucchinis and squash. He was the size of a small donkey! Interactions with wildlife are inevitable when you garden in the country, and although we try to keep our chickens safe, a fox got to them a while back. He was beautiful, like a fox from Central Casting—and he should have been, as he had eaten most of our chickens. But foxes do eat a lot of rodents, too.

Walking through our garden on a July afternoon, I feel sometimes that I am in a butterfly house, the butterflies are so pervasive. And as night falls, when I see the fireworks show the lightning bugs put on, it becomes very evident to me why I have a spray-free garden. These are experiences that money can't buy—you have to garden a certain way to get these effects. However, the deer are pushing the limits of my "we can all live happily together" philosophy. Last July, some lovely little spotted fawns and their kin ate just about every hosta in my garden. They munched on the daylilies, violas, sedums, Asian clethra, and some of the lilies. For years I'd relied on protecting my property by not planting deer food (for a deer, anything in the Liliaceae is an invitation to dinner) on the perimeter, and growing a lot of asters, including *Eurybia divaricata*, because the deer don't like them. I regularly applied deer repellents, which smell bad and presumably taste worse. But I knew that sooner or later I would face an all-out attack, and it has begun. After considering numerous options, I'm zoning in on a solar-powered single-strand fence, to be turned on at night. We shall see. For 300 years, we've been fighting the battle. Who's winning? The deer, I think.

The Veg at the heart of the garden

THE VEGETABLE GARDEN at Brandywine Cottage is center stage. Its central location is a matter of design, but philosophically it seems right that the heart of the garden should be The Veg. Growing vegetables is a reminder of what came first when we began tilling the soil—food. It speaks clearly of nature's abundance, and the relationship between nature and the gardener tending the earth. And it speaks directly to our agrarian roots, our own family history. I grew up with my grandparents' much larger vegetable garden, in the Great Smoky Mountains. I worked alongside them, picking beans, peas, corn, lettuce, strawberries. As many berries went into my mouth as into the collection bucket, but they never seemed to mind. I also went out foraging for blackberries with my friends. I wonder how many kids today can do that? And I can still taste my grandmother's blackberry cobbler, which was my reward. It was wonderful! These experiences gave me delightful memories, but more than that, they nurtured a love of plants that enhances every aspect of my life.

When you enter our property, the first thing you see as you walk down the drive is the vegetable garden. The windows in the rear of the house, on all three stories, look out over it. In a whimsical mood, you can almost envision the white picket fence around The Veg as the crown on top of the garden. But this space is a mingling of the practical and the ornamental. There is something very beautiful about utilitarianism, and I try to highlight that throughout the garden, but especially in The Veg. The overall design of the vegetable garden is four-square, which fits into the larger garden defined by the borders. Essentially, these larger and larger squares emanate outward from the vegetable garden, which has a square stone birdbath in the center. This care for the birds epitomizes our appreciation for all life, rippling out from The Veg to the larger garden and the woodland and wilds beyond.

above
The cold frame is used throughout the growing season.

Geometry is alive and
well in The Veg.

above
Sugar snap peas. Best eaten right off the vine.

above right
Bronze fennel is a soft yellow adored by me, the gardener, as well as by the larvae of black swallowtail butterflies. Remember: if you want to have the butterflies, you must first have the caterpillars.

We cultivate a variety of vegetables in The Veg, but we don't try to grow everything. We live close to Pennsylvania Dutch farm country, with easy access to farmers' markets, family produce stands, and local outlets for Community Supported Agriculture, so there's no need to grow crops like corn or potatoes. They require too much space. (I do admit to having grown some heirloom yams and sweet potatoes elsewhere in the garden, however.) This is not a garden intended to meet all our vegetable needs, but to augment our table and our lifestyle. Nothing perks up a dining experience so much as adding a little something that you grew. Whether it's early peas or heirloom tomatoes or preserved beets, that homegrown contribution raises the meal to a different level. Not only is there a sense of pride that you grew it yourself, you know how it was grown—in our case, entirely organically. It's one small way to have a positive impact on our own environment.

Although I did the original layout, Mike has taken the vegetable garden under his wing and is largely responsible for it. We select many of the plants together, but a lot of extras tend to follow me home. I generally place these offerings at the gate of The Veg, and it's fun to see how Mike positions them. Vegetables, annuals, perennials, herbs, and bulbs all grow in the vegetable garden, as we do not believe in segregating plants. I firmly believe that vegetable gardens can be ornamental as well as productive. As a result, we also consider color and height when it comes to choosing some of the vegetables. (Conversely, I will put vegetables in my perennial borders if I find them ornamental. Fennel, cotton, kale, okra, and countless herbs all play a part in my borders.) Several of the original plants, such as rhubarb, carex, and sorrel, still exist in the vegetable garden. These plants grow along the fence, since they are more or less perennial. The sorrel gets dangly in the summer, so is not a plant for center stage.

The garden changes in color from year to year because of the annuals we choose. Some years marigolds line the pathways, some years nasturtiums. It all depends on our mood. We also use containers in the vegetable garden—pots of lilies for seasonal color, combination pots of annuals and herbs, all are placed around The Veg with an eye to aesthetics. Mike recently added wooden half-barrels to the center of the four squares to give us raised gardens of sorts, in which we may grow tomatoes or pole beans. A rounded half-barrel in a square frame adds architectural interest as well. One consistent element in the vegetable garden is our use of bamboo teepees, which provide a vertical element. On those we grow climbers like pole beans, lima beans, and the annual *Lablab purpureus* (hyacinth bean), or sometimes sweet peas, for cutting. I use vertical forms—tall plants, rose tuteurs, trellises—throughout the entire garden to provide an upward lift. Drama! On the fence surrounding the vegetable garden, we grow at least seven different varieties of old or antique roses, which you can see from the borders or from inside the vegetable garden. It looks so beautiful, the roses spilling over the fence. This kind of plant diversity contributes to another layer of appreciation for nature at work in The Veg. Different plants offer more possibilities for pollinators. Birds build their nests in the rose bushes, and then eat insects on the plants to feed their young. Marigolds have insect-repelling qualities as well as being ornamental.

We put composted leaves on the vegetable beds each fall, and add composted cow manure every other year. We till this under each spring. Fresh salt hay (which has no weed seeds in it, unlike straw and feed hay) goes on the paths each spring, and perhaps later in the year as well; it suppresses weeds and keeps the paths from becoming muddy.

Each year is an experiment in gardening, but one of the nice things
about making mistakes in the vegetable garden is that if you don't like
how something is performing, you can almost always eat it. So what
are some of the edibles we grow? Lettuces of all kinds, both leaf and
head. Swiss chard, usually with colored leaves or stems. Cabbages of all
colors and varieties. Brussels sprouts. Beets. Kale, radishes, and early
peas. Watercress and carrots in containers. Tomatoes, both heirloom
and proven producers, plus cherry and other varieties. Bush and pole
beans—heirloom, stringless, and shelling—and shelling peas as well.
Leeks, chives, sweet onions, and green onions. Dill, basil, rosemary, sage.
Peppers, both sweet and hot. Eggplants, though not every year. Peas as a
summer crop. Cucumbers, squash, and zucchini. And some years we put
in melons, but usually they take up too much space.

YELLOW
MUSTARD
BEANS

INGREDIENTS

6 to 8 quarts yellow beans

8 tbsp prepared
   yellow mustard

3 cups vinegar

3 cups water

6 cups sugar

5 tsp salt

This is the month that vegetable gardens start churning out more produce than most gardeners know what to do with. In our kitchen garden, we have an abundance of beans. Time to start preparing some of that bounty to eat later.

Michael's mother, Eva Alderfer, is locally famous for her chow-chow, a traditional Pennsylvania Dutch recipe for pickled vegetables; it was in such demand that she began selling it. Michael uses one of her simpler pickling recipes to make Yellow Mustard Beans, but you can use any yellow beans—wax beans, pole beans, or bush beans. They all make a pretty presentation if you pickle them standing up in wide-mouth glass preserving jars. Serve the beans on a salad, with burgers, or as a tasty cold side dish with anything you like. Michael suggests throwing some sausages on the grill and serving the beans on the side to make a perfect summer dinner—especially if you can eat at a picnic table in the garden.

METHOD

Sterilize the glass preserving jars and lids. Cook the beans until they are just tender (not mushy). Meanwhile, make the brine by stirring the mustard and the water together in a saucepan over medium heat, and gradually add the sugar, salt, and vinegar. Bring to a brisk boil, then reduce heat to simmer. Place the cooked beans upright in the jars, and ladle hot brine over beans until liquid is half an inch from the top of each jar. Remove any bubbles. Seal snugly with lids, and process in boiling water bath for about 10 minutes, then remove with tongs and allow to cool before storing. Popping sounds as jars cool indicate that the jars have sealed properly.

opposite
Yellow Mustard Beans taste great
and look attractive on the plate.

AUGUST

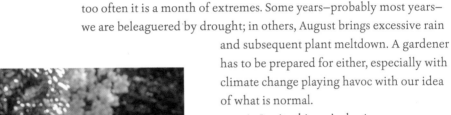

AUGUST TESTS A GARDENER'S SKILL and ingenuity. All too often it is a month of extremes. Some years—probably most years—we are beleaguered by drought; in others, August brings excessive rain and subsequent plant meltdown. A gardener has to be prepared for either, especially with climate change playing havoc with our idea of what is normal.

As I write this, we're having a summer of ample rain, and my garden looks lush and maybe a bit blowsy—a word I happen to like, whether it's used in reference to people or gardens. I can appreciate a woman in a blowsy hat as much as I can a woman in a tailored suit. Both are beautiful. And that is true of the garden in its ripeness—or in drought. The wild garden itself looks blowsy in August, so if we are taking our cue from nature, why not our own attempts? Should every season be the same?

Of necessity, Brandywine Cottage was built around the idea of water-wise gardening. I learned in my first year that the property's working well, with water about 360 feet down, could not support more than 1½ hours of irrigation with a hand-held hose. As housing developments grew up around me, those wells drew from the same aquifer, and my water levels dropped further. So I came to water-wise gardening as a practical approach—I really had no choice. As time passed, I noticed that a weeks-long mid-summer drought was common; often, rain in the region seemed to go north or south of our immediate vicinity. You know it's

above
August keeps you busy. Being a referee (keeping plants from overrunning one another) is part of the game plan.

opposite
Cornus kousa fruit.

dry when you find yourself cheering on tropical storms, urging them up the East Coast in hopes of a little rainfall. But as gardeners we must take what nature throws at us and make a garden. Luckily for me, I favor a Mediterranean palette, and many native plants also do well here, having adapted over centuries to dry summers and cold winters.

I am glad that my garden soil contains clay. It's not as bad as the dense Georgia clay I used to garden in, but I like it *because* it holds water. All I have to do is add leaf mold, constantly, to make it friable and fertile. Leaf mold is my go-to soil amendment and fertilizer. I don't use a lot of chemical fertilizers; they burn plants when I cannot water them in sufficiently, and too much nitrogen encourages rapid but weak growth. Most of my garden is on a very thin diet. I don't overfertilize, and I water only to get plants established. After that they are on their own—except for those in containers.

But whether the month is wet or dry, August brings home the importance of texture. The bodacious tropicals continue to play a major role in holding the border together, and they are supported in this effort by tall natives like Joe-Pye weed (*Eupatorium*) and ironweed (*Vernonia*). The biennial *Angelica gigas*, with its broad foliage and reddish purple stems topped by purple flower umbels, picks up similar tones in the banana, the purple perilla, and the phlox, creating a pleasing color echo. Umbels add horizontal planes to the border and impart a sense of naturalism; the trend toward naturalistic plantings has made them increasingly popular in recent years.

Dahlias are another staple of the summer garden that aren't hardy here in zone 7. But dahlias are such cheerful flowers, and perfect "over the fence" garden plants. For years, Michael and I have been swapping tubers with our friend Queenie Northrop, and we all visit specialty growers together. As you can imagine, we have collected many dahlias, and they produce abundant flowers from August to frost. Not only do they make great cut flowers, but the plants benefit from being cut. It encourages stronger plants and more flowers.

I divide the tubers as necessary each spring before I replant them, in late April or early May, which coincides with our last frost dates. Tall dahlias, or those with big flowers, generally require staking to prevent

left
Perennials and tropicals standing up against the hot summer sun. Tropicals add structure to an otherwise blowsy border.

their falling over, either from their own weight or in wind or rain. I have found that putting stakes in place when you plant the tubers saves time—and a lot of aggravation and disappointment later on, should you neglect this step. It allows the developing foliage to camouflage the stakes and also ensures that you won't damage a growing plant by accidentally putting the stake through the tuber. Some years, we use selected color forms in the borders; the bold and prolific dahlia foliage helps hold the "summer loose" borders together, visually. And we always have a few in The Veg.

above
Some of the diverse colors and shapes of dahlias, a mainstay of the garden in August and September.

opposite
Angelica gigas has lovely purple stems and, eventually, umbels. Pollinators seem to love it.

Gardens that look particularly good in August usually have a large number of annuals. This is a good idea for keeping the garden going in the summer doldrums, and often into fall. Salvia, penta, nicotiana, cleome, celosia—the list of possibilities goes on and on. These colorful flowers enhance the perennial plantings and bring both flowers *and* texture to the summer border. *Nicotiana sylvestris* has large leaves and long, trumpet-shaped flowers that are also fragrant, and *N. langsdorffii* contributes large, sticky leaves and nodding flowers of an unusual pale green. Simply replace your annuals each year from seed.

I rely on *Phlox paniculata* in the main border and *Rudbeckia hirta* (black-eyed Susan) in the south border to give me a big color boost in August. These plants self-sow almost to the point of being a nuisance and give me not only bright color but numerous flowers for arrangements.

above
You can count on *Rudbeckia hirta* for nonstop color in hot summer months.

above right
An August arrangement of hydrangeas and lilies.

opposite
Cornus controversa 'Variegata' stands out against the sea of green that dominates this time of year.

In summer the wealth of rudbeckias and other composite flowers seems to reflect the mood of the season—sunny, happy, and carefree. They have the same upbeat effect when you use them in arrangements indoors, or in a small vase on a taboret. Not only are they excellent fillers in arrangements, but they make people smile.

I could easily have a garden full of hydrangeas, many of which flower in June, July, and especially in August. It's the white-flowering ones, including the panicle hydrangeas, that do so much for the garden at this time of year, especially *Hydrangea paniculata* 'Tardiva'. White in the summer is so cooling. That's why people wear white at this time of year—it's cool, crisp, and clean-looking. I use hydrangeas in arrangements and containers as well as in the garden; often, when one has outgrown its usefulness in a container on the patio, it finds new life elsewhere in the garden—in the borders or at the forest edge.

As they do in any season, variegated trees and shrubs add color and interest to the garden in high summer, particularly when not much is flowering. The *Cornus controversa* 'Variegata', like a prima ballerina in a tutu, certainly takes center stage on the hillside. I first fell in love with this stunning variegated dogwood at Beth Chatto's garden in England many years ago. I often think of her when I look at

it—a treasured memory. It's rewarding how plants do that, bring back old friends. I do caution about too much variegation, however. It can easily be overdone. There's pretty variegation, even pretty random variegation, but not all variegation is attractive to me. I use it as an accent—I like it to look as though it is intentional, rather than something the pigeons roosted above. I also have a tall variegated pokeweed (*Phytolacca americana*), and if I could find a big enough variegated devil's walking stick (*Aralia spinosa*), I'd be tempted to put that at one end of a border. Both are natives.

People are surprised that I grow pokeweeds—I have the golden variety, too—but I find them attractive for their foliage and for the berries they produce in autumn, and they are versatile in arrangements. They do seed around if you let them, however, so buyer beware. A firm

hand is needed if you decide to use plants like this that have an ebullient nature. I like the challenge of using, in a formal way, a plant that most people consider a weed—pokeweed, say, or even something like chicory (*Cichorium intybus*). I'm like a plant coach, helping this plant to reach its potential in the garden. Success depends on where the plant is placed, and how it is used. That means using it in a different context from the one in which most people see it. I don't see chicory just as something growing in a roadside ditch, for example—I see its possibilities with other companions and other colors, such as an orange poppy or butterfly weed (*Asclepias tuberosa*). After all, one man's weed is another man's treasure. Many self-sowers act like the stitchery that knits a garden together, giving continuity to a design; that's how I think of both corydalis and comfrey (*Symphytum*), as enthusiastic groundcovers in dry spots.

But if you have a garden, weeds—the ones you don't want—are just one aspect of what I think of as gardening realism. Favorite plants are going to die. Deer or some other critters are going to dine on prized shrubs. Weather will wreak havoc. Things happen in a garden. It's not a static art form, and isn't that in some ways what we like? We just have to look at these happenings in different ways. I have always felt that in order to enjoy a garden fully, it helps to be a gardener—that is, someone who appreciates the work that has gone into it.

Luckily, I like to weed. That's a good thing, because the ruin garden needs a lot of weeding and cutting back in a hot and humid summer. I used to have more visible stone, but now it's much more wild, richer and fuller. It takes a while to learn how far you can let the plants go. I do like contemporary lines, but I also like nature. When I look at this garden, and then at photos of a more contemporary garden, I think, *How sterile!* The ruin garden is more approachable, which is what I want in a garden. Yes, there are a lot of unusual plants here, but I want the overall experience to be comfortable. It's a garden, not a landscape.

Water-wise plants for dry places

HERE IS A LIST OF PLANTS that I consider water-wise. This is the term I have always used, although gardening that reduces or eliminates the need for supplemental watering is now often known as xeriscaping. However you refer to it, the goal is the same—to save water. And these plants have worked for me.

Acanthus. Bold texture. Several species are hardy in the mid-Atlantic states. Produces handsome, hooded flowers on 4-foot stalks in June. The leaves are the inspiration for the capitals of Corinthian columns.

Achillea millefolium. Yarrow tolerates drought and heat like a champion. Deer and rabbit resistant. Comes in a variety of colors, though mostly yellow. Full sun, well-drained soils.

Allium. Very useful bulbs, in a multitude of heights, sizes, and bloom times. Almost all feature a spherical or loosely spherical flowerhead.

Artemisia. Indispensable for gray foliage effect. In rainy summers, however, some artemisias may melt (i.e., the foliage becomes soft and disintegrates). Nevertheless, the gray foliage is irresistible. I think of them in two basic groups, clumpers or runners.

Arum italicum subsp. *italicum* '**Marmoratum**'. Tuberous perennial. I grow it for its mottled leaves that appear right after the berries vanish in late summer. At least three seasons of interest. Sorry for readers who live in Oregon, where it is considered invasive. Not for me! Shade tolerant.

Asphodeline lutea. Narrow, grassy-like foliage, 3- to 4-foot flower spikes topped by yellow flowers. Easily grown in full sun and average to well-drained soils. Hardy to zone 6.

Calamintha nepeta. Light green, deer-resistant, mint-scented; airy plumes of barely blue flowers. Extra-long bloom period.

Campanula portenschlagiana. One of the most popular bellflowers. Very small and very vigorous. Great for rock walls and crevices.

Cardoons and cynaras. Large, gray-green, thistle-like leaves lend architectural splendor to these plants, which are topped by purple thistle-like

above
Asphodeline lutea.

opposite
Achillea millefolium, with *Verbena bonariensis* and *Onopordum acanthium*, all suitable for dry conditions.

flowers in mid-summer. Can reach up to 4 or 5 feet. Full sun. Hardy to zone 7, but worth growing as an annual.

Crambe. *Crambe maritima* (sea kale) tolerates dry, well-drained soils. It has glaucous leaves and white flowers in umbels, but I use it mostly for its bold texture. *Crambe cordifolia* grows to 6 feet tall, with clouds of white flowers in June. I use it exclusively for floral effect, usually in the back of the border, because its foliage is often eaten by bugs.

Cyclamen. These plants, with their gorgeous patterned leaves, are perfect for the cottage, because they demand a dry, well-drained situation. I position them among rocks or up against a tree trunk, where it's dry. More cyclamen have been killed by overwatering than by anything else. The flowers are icing on the cake: *C. coum* begins flowering in early spring, *C. purpurascens* in summer, and *C. hederifolium* in fall. Hardy to at least zone 6.

above
Echinops bannaticus 'Blue Globe'.

above right
Euphorbia griffithii 'Dixter'.

Echinops. Globe thistles produce round, metallic-blue flowerheads, which are great for drying. Very easy to grow.

Ephedra. A genus of clump-forming plants, native to the Southwest. Architectural. Glaucous to green stems, gray foliage. I give mine well-drained soil in the rock garden, and it has been a talking point for 15 years. Criminally underused. Hardy to zone 7.

Euphorbia. Love 'em, love 'em, love 'em. Euphorbias offer diversity of height, foliage color, flower color, and habit. Their mostly evergreen foliage and drought tolerance make them very useful. The flowers (bracts) are very distinctive; I love their color and shape. Rabbits and deer won't eat euphorbias; their milky sap is poisonous. Many people have a dermatological reaction to the sap. I didn't, until a few years ago, but now I get a rash. Wear gloves!

Eurybia divaricata. Clouds of white flowers are lovely, especially when this fall-blooming native aster is naturalized. Tolerant of dry rocky soils, grows in part shade to full shade. A must for the woodland garden. Deer resistant.

Galtonia. This summer-flowering bulb offers beautiful white flowers in early August. Zone 7; may overwinter in mild winters.

Gaura. From the Southwest. Drought tolerant. Lighter soils help in overwintering. Hundreds of tiny white flowers dangle like small butterflies on almost invisible stems.

Hellebores. Stalwart and charming performers in the part shade/dry shade garden. Color possibilities are almost limitless. Certainly the queen of the winter garden.

Iris. Many, many iris prefer hot, baking growing conditions.

Kniphofia. If you thought kniphofias came only in red, think again. Many new color forms are available, as well as repeat flowering ones. Dislikes overcrowding.

Lavenders. Signature plants for full sun, best in well-drained soils. They scream "Mediterranean"—and have a wonderful fragrance, too.

Mine are in 50 percent gravel. Poor drainage and winter wet kill these, not cold.

Liatris. Vertical element in the garden. Vibrant purple flowers from late June (*L. spicata*) through early fall (*L. microcephala, L. squarrosa, L. scariosa*). Pollinators love them.

Nepeta. Beautiful yet utilitarian. If you've given up on growing lavenders, try nepeta. Easy maintenance. The shorter cultivars have become very popular.

Opuntia humifusa. Eastern prickly pear is a clump-forming hardy cactus bearing yellow flowers and reddish fruits. This showy native cactus has a wide distribution. Aside from the barbed bristles (which really hurt—handle with thick gloves), I don't know why it isn't more widely used.

Oregano. Requires dry conditions to grow well. Ornamental and herbal uses. It is a beautiful plant when well grown.

Patrinia scabiosifolia. Easy to grow. Long bloom time; sprays or panicles of bright yellow flowers in summer, when you really need color. Full sun. Grows 3 to 6 feet tall. Good cut flower. Should be more widely grown.

above
This red hot poker is bright yellow.

above middle
Liatris squarrosa.

above right
Opuntia humifusa.

opposite
Iris 'Quaker Lady' with an early-blooming salvia.

Although once a suspected host of daylily rust, this has never been proven. I grow both it and daylilies with no ill effects.

Perovskia atriplicifolia. Russian sage is the standard-bearer of drought-tolerant perennials. Blooms for many weeks, lavender-blue flowers over silver-gray foliage. Deer and rabbit resistant, too! They won't touch it.

Poppies. Most of those grown from seed do wonderfully in dry conditions. Very useful self-sower.

Rohdea japonica. Sacred lily, an evergreen perennial with strappy green leaves, makes an elegant groundcover or specimen that withstands shade, drought, and deer. Almost tropical-looking and yet it is hardy in our garden, and probably to zone 5 with a little protection. Another underused plant.

Rubus. Ghost brambles are great for winter interest, when the gray stems are used to striking effect. Some cultivars have yellow foliage. Not for the polite perennial border: plants tend to gallop through the garden. Best used in disturbed sites.

Salvia. All-around good plants that grow in a variety of conditions. Salvias in general are the backbone of many annual plantings for summer and fall, but I have found the perennial and the herbal types to be the most drought-tolerant. One is tempted to have them all.

Sedums. Tall sedums are useful in perennial borders or as specimen plants. Dwarf sedums are a popular groundcover. Sedums require full sun. Widely used for roof gardens.

Sempervivum. "Live forever" indeed. I remember my grandmother growing hens-and-chicks, but they have become very chic again. Their foliage is architectural, on a small scale. Grow in troughs, on rooftops, in containers. Plants thrive on full sun, poor soils—and neglect.

Stachys. Many people think of *S. byzantina* (lamb's ear) with its woolly silver foliage when they think of drought-tolerant stachys, and they are right to do so, but I have found it problematic in wet summers. *Stachys officinalis* (betony), a green-leafed vertical plant with violet-pink flowers, is very easy to grow; my favorite is *S. officinalis* 'Hummelo'.

Symphyotrichum cordifolium. Clouds of blue aster flowers in early fall. Does well at the woodland's edge and in dry meadows. Will grow in dry shade, and under walnut trees, where it resists the toxin juglone. Deer resistant.

above
Sempervivums—you may know them as hens-and-chicks.

above right
Symphyotrichum cordifolium.

Thymus. Many colors. Useful in full-sun areas and rock gardens. Common choice for planting between pavers. Very European.

Verbascum. *Verbascum thapsus, V. chaixii*, and *V. ×hybridum* are short-lived perennials. Great vertical accents to 6 feet tall. Grow well in poor soils and often self-sow in full sun on dry, rocky slopes.

Yucca. Relatively large succulent-looking plants that provide an architectural element. Many species are native to the Southwest; those that are hardy for us come from high altitudes in Arizona and Utah.

above
Verbascum with alliums.

above right
Yucca, standing tall.

SUMMER SQUASH PIZZA

This pizza is Michael's interpretation of a recipe a friend found online. He uses a mandoline to slice the squash, which gives it a much more attractive appearance and allows even cooking; depending on the blade used, a mandoline can also give the slices a pretty, slightly wavy edge. Serve this pizza with a mixed green salad—featuring produce from your vegetable garden, if possible—for a colorful and satisfying late-summer supper.

INGREDIENTS

1 cup ricotta cheese

½ tsp garlic salt

½ tsp herbs (oregano, rosemary, sage) or Italian seasoning

¼ tsp red pepper flakes

About 10 large basil leaves, finely chopped

Summer squash, green and/or yellow, as you prefer; each about 8 inches long and similar in diameter

2 tsp salt

12-inch prebaked thin pizza crust (store-bought or previously made)

Olive oil for drizzling

Black pepper

METHOD

In a medium-size bowl, combine ricotta, garlic salt, herbs/seasoning, red pepper flakes, and chopped basil. Set aside.

Slice the squash into rounds about ⅛ inch thick. Put the slices in a colander set over a bowl, toss with salt, and let them sit for about 15 minutes. The salt helps the squash release liquid. Then, spread the slices on one half of an absorbent kitchen towel, fold the other half over the squash, and press down evenly to absorb as much moisture as possible.

Position a rack in the center of the oven. Preheat oven to 400 degrees Fahrenheit.

Place the pizza crust on a rimless baking sheet, and spread the ricotta mixture over the crust, leaving a ½-inch border. Arrange the squash slices, slightly overlapping, over the cheese. Alternate green and yellow slices, or different colored circles, as desired. Drizzle the surface with olive oil and a dusting of coarsely ground black pepper.

Slide the pizza directly onto the central oven rack, and bake until the crust is crisp and the squash just starting to brown, 15 to 20 minutes. Slide the cooked pizza from the oven rack back onto the baking sheet, then onto a wooden cutting board. Let it sit for 5 or 6 minutes, and slice into wedges.

opposite
Summer Squash Pizza will taste even better if you can serve it to friends al fresco.

GROUND CHERRY PIE

Ground Cherry Pies are so treasured, they are sometimes raffled off as prizes at pie sales in Pennsylvania Dutch regions. People often freeze them and save them for special occasions. This recipe is from Michael's mother, Eva Alderfer.

Ground Cherry Pies are so treasured, they are sometimes raffled off as prizes at pie sales in Pennsylvania Dutch regions. People often freeze them and save them for special occasions. This recipe is from Michael's mother, Eva Alderfer.

The ground cherry plant, Physalis pruinosa, *is in the family Solanaceae, along with tomatoes, eggplants, and potatoes. Common names include ground gooseberry, Cape gooseberry, and husk tomato—because the berries are wrapped in a papery husk that turns brownish when the berries are ripe. The berries themselves are a golden color and still fairly firm when ripe. I think they look rather like gooseberries. They taste sweet, like pineapple, strawberry, and mango all fused together.*

You can sometimes buy ground cherries at farmers' markets, but they are easy to grow yourself. Sow the seeds indoors 4 to 6 weeks before your last frost date, and plant them out, 18 to 24 inches apart, after frost is no longer likely. Put them in an area of the garden that you don't mind looking a little weedy, as the plants tend to sprawl. Mulch around the plants with straw or grass clippings to make fallen fruits easier to spot—and to prevent too many new seedlings from popping up. Ground cherries can be quite prolific.

INGREDIENTS

¼ cup table cream
(or light cream)

¼ cup Karo syrup

2 tbsp water

½ cup sugar

1 tbsp flour

2½ cups ground cherries
(husks removed)

9-inch pie crust

METHOD

Preheat oven to 400 degrees Fahrenheit. Mix cream, syrup, water, sugar, and flour together. Fill pie crust with the ground cherries, then pour the mixture over the ground cherries. Bake for 70 to 75 minutes, until golden brown. Serve warm or cold, with ice cream if desired.

opposite
Ground Cherry Pie is a Mennonite favorite, a dessert that is considered an extra special treat.

EARLY FALL

opposite
Ilex verticillata 'Afterglow' with
purple calla lilies.

SEPTEMBER

SEPTEMBER IS AN EASIER MONTH in the garden. The light changes, creating more shadows. The mood is softer than in August. The sun is lower in the sky. In the afternoon, its rays slant across the garden. This continues into November. The changeable light is one of the delightful things about autumn. There's a little crispness in the air in September, and, as I write this, a little moisture too. Plants like this. But only some years are like this!

Lobelias are blooming. After being seduced by the colors of many cultivars, I have concluded that the straight species, *Lobelia cardinalis* and *L. siphilitica*, are the most reliable. Sports of the two species do well. So, I stick with the species and their sports. The complex hybrids simply don't come back for me.

The colchicums attract attention wherever they are planted. It's almost as though someone has turned on a light within them. Although their beauty is singular, they look best combined with other plants. At the very least, give them a green background. I grow several species. They start blooming in early September and continue until October, depending on the species or cultivar. Colchicums do best at the woodland's edge and other areas that are not too shady. In spring, they produce large green leaves that are handsome in their own right, though they can be unsightly as they go over. Every year when the colchicums are in bloom I try to remember to plant more; they look better when planted in groups, or left undisturbed for decades and allowed to increase in size. I look at them in late September and appreciate the fact that they are deer-proof, especially after the hostas are long gone. You should buy them when you can get them! They come in pink, purple, white, and lavender, in single and double flower forms.

Sedums and September go together. Sedums come in many forms, but *Hylotelephium spectabile*, the species behind the long-lived Autumn Joy sedum, is probably the standard-bearer. The Atropurpureum Group

of *H. telephium* is also important, giving us some bronzy/purple foliage to work with; the bronze leaves look good with gray-foliage plants, or, for those among us who like a bolder combination, with yellow-foliage plants. To control flopping, you can pinch back your sedums earlier in the season, or you can stake them. I prefer pinching. This must be done in late May or June, to allow the plants time to grow and set bloom for the autumn. I stake very little in the garden, but there are times you have to. I prefer not to see the stakes. I don't want to show any artificial effect, especially in the perennial border, so I'm more inclined to take the pinching route—or to let the plant flop and call it grace. If your sedums start flopping over, it may be that they need to be divided, or you may be growing them in too much shade or soil that is too rich.

Sedums have become very popular, both dwarf and tall varieties. They are useful in borders, containers, and on green roofs. In fact, they are extremely practical in any water-wise garden. Sedums were some of my earliest plantings at Brandywine Cottage, because the first garden I put in was the roof garden. The roof of my house is cedar shake, and I knew the part over the porch back then was on the downside of its life. If it's going to have a swan song, I figured, it should be a pretty one—so I proceeded to plant it right away, plugging in dwarf sedums and sempervivums. It was while I was up on the roof doing this that I first met my neighbors. They asked what I was doing, and I responded that I was putting in a garden. They looked at me a little oddly. Playing with perspective has always been fun for me, so the roof was fertile ground in more than one way. Over the next few years I added opuntias and *Iris tectorum* (roof iris) and seeded some bleeding hearts in the shady areas. Ferns also rooted in. That roof garden lasted for many years, until I had to replace the roof itself. I vowed I wouldn't hasten the new roof's demise to accommodate a garden, but I did decide that when it started to look venerable, I would plant. So, in the last few years, I've started over where I began, creating a roof garden. Michael and my friends have made me promise that I won't go out on the roof unless somebody else is in the garden, in case I fall off. The roof can get quite slippery. But I

like to sit out there, on a little ledge, and look out over my garden from a bird's-eye perspective. Give me a roof, or a rock wall, or a black walnut tree, and I'll give you a garden. It's the visual perspective that I find exciting, and I'm constantly experimenting everywhere in the garden. I enjoy the challenge.

Salvias come into their own in September. *Salvia farinacea* is a workhorse of an annual, a reliable filler, and much happier when planted in drifts with perennials rather than in a straight line. It blooms from summer until frost. I put it into the garden in June, when we do our plant change-out. Salvias have become very popular recently, what with the increasing emphasis on late-summer and fall gardening—so many more species and cultivars from which to choose, with all kinds of color nuances that we didn't have 20 years ago, and a greater range of heights. There is just so much on offer for those who are willing to seek it out.

Begonia grandis (hardy begonia) is now covered with flowers, which always seems a bit of a surprise in our garden at this time of year. Late bloom *and* it is hardy to zone 6. The problem is that the deer like it as much as I do. In an effort to thwart them, I grow it in different spots, hoping that they will miss one spot and leave it for me. This begonia is very easy to grow in part shade, and very easy to divide; its flowers are pink or, less commonly, white. Joanna Reed gave me a piece of it, years ago, and in the entry garden are rain lilies (*Zephyranthes candida*), which I got from Susie Novoa, Joanna's daughter. So as I walk toward my front door, I'm greeted by friends. Gardening is like that, about memories as well as plants. All those precious little gifts that are pressed into your hands by people who say, "You've got to have this!"—nine times out of ten, they're right.

above

From the September garden, clockwise from top left: callicarpa; solidago; tree peony seedpod; *Verbascum chaixii* seedhead; agastache seedhead; *Clinopodium nepeta*; Autumn Joy sedum seedhead; *Salvia farinacea* spent flower.

Nicotianas are blooming in September, and the ones I cut back in summer are reblooming. The last couple of years, I planted tobacco (*Nicotiana tabacum*) in the borders and in the meadow. Unlike other nicotianas I grow, its tubular flowers are not the main draw; what I love is the height and texture it provides. The meadow is about pollinators, which is why I'm also growing mountain mint (*Pycnanthemum muticum*) near the beehives. It flowers from summer to early fall and is an excellent source of nectar for many types of pollinators. I used this in another meadow I designed, and it was so fragrant that strolling through the meadow was like walking in a mint julep. I'm also growing *Stewartia pseudocamellia* Koreana Group, but I've used different seedlings and different sizes to make it look like they have sown themselves out there. Friends say this may not be in character with a native meadow, but it's not just about being native; it's about being sustainable and about having fun with color.

In the ruin garden, I'm continuing to experiment with my color palette. I've gotten away from bright colors for the moment and am now going for a more tonal look. I've noticed myself using a lot more Mediterranean blues and grays, but it's subtle and needs a few accent colors here and there.

I feel like I'm the East Coast experimental station for hardy cactus, and I'm trying some of them in the ground instead of in containers. Space is limited in the ruin garden, so I make little planting pockets in addition to the pots and hypertufa troughs. That's the joy of containers,

you can amend the soil—though I don't recommend it in the larger garden: if you dig a hole in clay and try to play with the soil in that space, it becomes a container that holds water. I've replaced some of the troughs at the rear of the garden with a large, shallow sink raised up on the base of an old Singer sewing machine. It's something different, but I think it goes well with the design of the garden.

There's a thin line between being a collector of plants, and housing your collections in a garden setting. In my opinion, collections and aesthetics don't have to be mutually exclusive. I try to use my many collections in a garden context rather than as a botanical display. I've done one thing differently that makes most rock garden people cringe, and that is to use a couple of tropical plants. But why not? We do it in the larger garden, and I needed a vertical. If it works in my design, in it goes. One thing about rock gardening—you can do more interesting plants per square inch than anywhere else in the garden. If you live in the city, or you have only a patio, but you still want to have a botanic garden look, you can do it with rock garden plants and have a world-class garden in a small space.

I like unusual plants, including the recently introduced *Calycanthus floridus* var. *purpureus* 'Burgundy Spice'. Unlike other native sweetshrubs, it has purple foliage—a dramatic color change. As a bonus, in autumn it turns lovely shades of orange and yellow. But I think *Solanum quitoense* (bed-of-nails), a subtropical perennial from South America, may steal the show when it is part of a display. It has large leaves, with wicked-looking spikes along its leaf veins and stems, and ball-shaped fruit that are covered in stinging hairs—making it another of my anti-social plants, a description that could also include thistles, agaves, and prickly pear cactus. These are plants that evoke an emotional response that goes beyond the visual. The response to this solanum might be "Ouch!" But the idea is to use different plants or design elements (stepping stones through a water feature, for instance) to entice people to participate more intensely with the garden, rather than just looking. Interactions like these deepen people's involvement with gardens.

I enjoy a multi-dimensional garden. The halesia bed, behind the ruin garden, is a quiet, peaceful space at this time of year, with a bench inviting a visitor to sit a while and meditate. But it is also an obsessive-compulsive's delight, because I love weeding the moss. It's just like editing. The monks do this in Japan, too, and it is so satisfying. This is a time for weeding out and cutting back in general, but many of these

trimmings can take on new life as arrangements. And if some of the leaves have a hole or two from nibbling insects, isn't that part of nature? I once visited the garden of Prince Charles in England, and one of the people I was with said, "What a beautiful garden. But what a shame it isn't up to American standards of maintenance." The prince's garden is organic, and so there were some chewed leaves. That got me thinking, what is beautiful? Chewed leaves are natural. A dehiscing leaf is natural. Spent flowers are natural. I think a garden with some chewed leaves is beautiful, because it is about life.

My favorite weeds

IF YOU ARE GOING to have a garden, you are going to have weeds. They are a fact of life in gardening. And if you are going to have weeds, you might as well have ones that are pretty, or useful, or both. Think of the weeds you like as super-sowers that can cover bare ground, provide a dramatic talking point, or fill in some glaring hole in the garden.

What follows is a list of my favorite weeds, and why I like them. To what extent I let them survive depends on the year, my intent, and, truth be told, my mood. But they are not allowed to crowd out their neighbors. When they start overrunning, I start ripping them out, wholesale. You can do that with these plants because you have the luxury of abundance; you won't miss them.

***Ageratina altissima* 'Chocolate'**. Although I enjoy this perennial's white flowers and purple foliage, its ability to seed itself around proves that sometimes enough is enough. I always weed out the reversions: I don't mind that 'Chocolate' is a super-sower as much as I mind that it reverts to a muddy or green-leafed form.

***Corydalis lutea*.** I fell in love with this plant several decades ago at a garden center. But I put it in too much shade and near a downspout, and the excessive wetness killed it. So I bought three more, and I still have the progeny of those plants. Corydalis seeds itself around with great abandon, and I doubt you could come up with a list of many perennials that bloom as long as this one. It begins in spring, rests only in the hottest spots of summer, and continues into fall.

How can you resist a plant that does that? It pops up in the most curious places, including stone walls and gravel paths. It moves willingly into dry places that need some color, so it is a good addition to my Mediterranean palette. Its very watery stems are a breeze to pull out. Visitors and passersby never fail to notice it and ask for a bit—like many of the "weeds" on this list. By late September, I'll go through and rip it out. It will be back.

Euphorbia cyparissias. Cypress spurge is tolerant of poor soils, even rocky or sandy ones. It has beautiful yellow flowers in April and May. It makes a dense groundcover in full sun and takes very dry conditions, spreading readily by underground rhizomes, which can be a problem. I probably wouldn't use it in a perennial border, but it's great at the edges of the garden and out in the rock garden by the road. There, I have underplanted it with tulips, and so far it has kept the rabbits from eating the tulips.

Geranium. Herb Robert (*G. robertianum*) is a very small, sweet-looking geranium. Most people grow the pink or magenta color, but I think it is worth seeking out the white form, which scrambles around the garden, creating a unified appearance. Geraniums are deservedly very popular plants, and many are indispensable in the border, such as *G. phaeum* var. *phaeum* 'Samobor', which quickly displayed a willingness to seed around everywhere. It is nevertheless an attractive plant that can be quite useful

above
Corydalis lutea is very long-blooming and happy to insert itself into spots all over the garden. However, it is easy to pull out.

above right
Geranium phaeum var. *phaeum* 'Samobor'.

if controlled. Herb Robert I grow informally, in transition areas, the rock garden, the woodland's edge. Again, it is easy to pull out.

Matteuccia struthiopteris. Ostrich fern is a very popular circumboreal native. When I first started the garden, this species was given to me as a gift. Three plants. What the giver didn't tell me is how vigorous it is. Its attributes include tall green fronds, both fertile and infertile, fiddleheads that are edible—and it does spread. Realize if you plant it that it will cover a lot of ground, even growing into the crowns of other plants. In hot summers and droughts, it burns to a crisp. Sometimes it is just halfway crisped, which is probably even worse because then you have to cut it back. It makes you long for a rainy summer. Eventually, I basically caved and gave the ostrich fern a bed to itself, along the drive, but I am vigilant about monitoring its attempts to move elsewhere. When visitors see all the ferns along my driveway, they say how beautiful and cool it looks. But I pull out about a hundred each year as they try to get into the hellebores, the Solomon's seal, and anything else nearby. I even pull it away from newly established shrubs lest it shade them out.

Phacelia bipinnatifida. This little native plant has beautiful spotted foliage and lovely blue flowers, somewhat resembling geraniums. I had seen it on woodland walks, not knowing what it was, and then someone gave me one. I planted it halfway down the hillside. Since then it has sown itself all the way down and into the garden. I have to watch that it doesn't overrun some perennials, but it is so beautiful when it blooms in spring. You can move seedlings easily—but it will move around where and as it wishes, too. It grows 18 to 24 inches tall and tends to be a biennial, so don't pull it all out. Pennsylvania and south seems to be its native range; it is used to stunning effect at Mt. Cuba in Delaware.

Phlox paniculata. Everyone is all about native plants, and I am too, but many are weedy as well. *Phlox paniculata* is one such plant. About 25 years ago, I put in some selections of *P. paniculata*, including 'David' and 'Robert Poore'. They all crossed one hot summer night, and these hybrids now cover a large part of my main border. Even when I cut off the seedheads, a few always

above

Phlox paniculata. I count on it for its color—and because pollinators adore it.

above right

Phytolacca americana berries.

manage to escape and sow themselves elsewhere. So, we weed them out all spring long, trying to tame their exuberance. Students or interns who work in the garden generally have a slight dislike of phlox because plants are tougher to pull out. But if there's even a bit of powdery mildew on a plant, out it goes. Because of this, I'm getting a pretty good mildew-resistant strain going—not a big surprise, because 'David' and 'Robert Poore' are two of the better resistant cultivars. Phlox are not polite sowers; they put themselves in the crowns of other plants and shade them out, eventually killing them—which is why you have to control the phlox. Even a native plant as beautiful as this can be a problem. Sometimes I think it is trying to take over the world.

Phytolacca americana. Pokeweed. I've known it and weeded it all my life. I like the foliage and the berries, both of which provide vivid fall color. The berries are very attractive, a deep purplish black when ripe, and a food source for many birds. In the Revolutionary War, soldiers crushed them to make ink to write to loved ones. As a child I tried to do the same; it worked, vaguely. I have a variegated form and a gold-leaf form from Wave Hill in New York, anchoring each end of the border, but even these seed around like the straight species (and a certain percentage of seedlings revert to green). These weeds almost look like small trees in my garden. Most people who come by say, "I didn't know they could grow that tall!" But if you don't want that, you can cut them back hard in June, say, and they will grow again, but stay smaller. When you want to get rid of them altogether, you have to pull them out by the root—and they have a long taproot. To share, I dig out the seedlings when they are 6 to 8 inches tall, to keep the taproot intact, or else they won't survive. I like to use pokeweed in arrangements, too; initially, the stems wilt, but within 24 hours they become turgid again. Warning: pokeweed is poisonous to people and pets—especially the roots, berries and seeds—but even the leaves can be toxic.

Pulmonaria. A genus in the Boraginaceae, along with symphytums. Pulmonarias are good for the shade garden and tolerate dry conditions. In the '90s they achieved cult status, and as it was my job—and my passion—to find new plants that had desirable characteristics for ornamental horticulture, I tried too many of the many new cultivars in my garden. They did a lot of crossing, and seeded around more than I expected. Their offspring still come up everywhere, so I weed them out where I don't want them. They aren't particularly difficult to pull up, but they, too, will crowd out hellebores and other less-vigorous neighbors because their leaves are so dense. On the plus side, those leaves are fuzzy, so the deer tend not to bother them.

Purple perilla. I'm in love with the color purple and use it extensively in the garden. So when someone gave me a purple perilla, I thought it was perfect for me. However, they did not tell me how it sowed around. And I mean, it sowed around! It is truly the gift that keeps on giving. I've been weeding it out for 20 years or more, and I can't seem to get rid of it. My

approach now is that I'll always have it, so I just pull it out where I don't want it, or plant on top of it and treat it shabbily. If it's overshadowing the plant next to it, I rip it out without a qualm. I may curse at it when I'm weeding, but it's easy to pull out. And in the garden, its reddish purple leaves are still pretty. Some use the young leaves in salads, to add a little flounce of color and flavor. However, farmers would never allow perilla to grow in their pastures; it is toxic to horses and ruminants, including cattle.

Rudbeckia hirta. Black-eyed Susan has naturalized everywhere, from meadows to ditches. It also self-seeds freely in the garden, so you may want to deadhead it if it becomes too rambunctious—or you can cut the showy flowers to make lots of bouquets. Like *Phlox paniculata*, it is indispensable for summer color. Very easy to grow in medium- to well-drained soils, and great for casual plantings and cottage gardens, blooming from July to September. Usually, it will grow and flower from seed within a year, though not necessarily the first fall, and it is low maintenance. It's a full-sun plant, so spreading into shade gardens is not a problem. Excess plants are pulled out fairly easily; I always have more than enough to share.

Symphytum. You may call *S.* 'Hidcote Blue' and *S. caucasicum* weedy; I call them great groundcovers for dry shade. I grow both in part shade and do they run! They'll grow where other things won't. It's their extreme willingness to live that makes them both a blessing and a challenge. If you grow them, make sure you give them plenty of room. They do tend to overrun their neighbors—plant them and step back. I always share symphytum with a warning, telling those who have asked for it not to come back and complain if it takes over their gardens or becomes a weed. The flowers themselves are charming: *S. caucasicum* is a clear blue, *S.* 'Hidcote Blue' is white with blue at the base. Many symphytums have herbal uses.

Violets/violas. What's not to love about a violet? They are so charming and sweet. Flowers are edible, too, and can be candied or used as

above

Symphytum caucasicum is a great groundcover for dry shade but likely to overrun what neighbors it has.

above right

Violets are charming little flowers for any part-shade area.

garnishes in salads. I don't put them in my perennial bed, but I use them along pathways and transition areas, at the edge of the woodland, and in the part-shade woodland garden. I don't mind if they sow around a bit—often in my water-wise garden I need something that will flourish. When they overgrow their bounds, I simply rip them out or cut them back. I have many different cultivars; they look so much more natural than pansies in my garden. What most people don't know is that many violets flower in the autumn as well, but we don't see the flowers because of the leaves. Fritillary butterflies like to lay their eggs on wild violets. Violets were wildly popular in Victorian times. And yet—once a garden visitor from out of state stood in my driveway, pointed to my violets, and said in a condescending tone, "I'm surprised you have these. We consider them weeds where I come from." I just looked at her and said, "You must have a very small garden, or else you don't like to weed." I'm not usually so blunt, but she was criticizing one of my children! That's one of the things about garden tours—what people say can be amazing.

BLACK WALNUT COOKIES

INGREDIENTS

1 cup butter

1 cup sugar

1 cup dark brown sugar

¾ tsp maple extract

2 eggs

3¼ cups flour

1 tsp baking soda

1 tsp salt

1½ cups chopped
black walnuts

One of my favorite cookies. Every year, I buy them at my Quaker Meeting's fall bake sale. The cookies for the bake sale are made by fellow member Jody Kinney, whose recipe this is; special thanks to her for sharing it. It's easy to follow, and the cookies are delicious. This recipe yields two dough logs for us, or about six dozen cookies. But if you don't want to bake all the cookies at once, freeze one log until you are ready to use it. It's great to have on hand in case of unexpected company.

We have two big black walnut trees growing behind the kitchen. Yes, the juglone toxin they produce makes it difficult to grow most plants beneath them; however, their delicious nuts are a decided benefit. Even if you don't have your own walnut tree, these cookies are well worth making with walnuts from the store.

METHOD

Preheat oven to 350 degrees Fahrenheit.

In a large bowl, cream the butter, white sugar, brown sugar, and maple extract. Add the eggs and beat until smooth.

Sift together the flour, baking soda, and salt. Stir the dry ingredients into the creamed mixture until well blended. Stir the walnuts in last.

Shape the dough into logs about 2 inches in diameter, wrap them in wax paper, and refrigerate until firm. Slice the logs into ¼-inch slices, and place them on a baking sheet. Bake for 8 to 10 minutes, or until cookies are lightly browned.

opposite
Black Walnut Cookies on a
redware plate.

OCTOBER

I DON'T THINK THERE IS ANY EXCUSE for the October garden to be dull. There are so many elements to choose from for color and drama—leaves, berries, late-season perennials and annuals, seedpods, and seasonal accents like gourds, pumpkins, and acorns. Although I love the first bright flowers of spring, I love the fall foliage colors even more.

Here in eastern North America, the colors of fall are like few other places in the world, which gives us an edge for spectacular fall gardens. Mother Nature is working in a warmer color palette in October, but she embraces pastels and jewel tones as well. Foliage takes center stage with the reds and golds of turning leaves, and I like to add bronze foliage to the richness of the season. But don't discount the flowers of the fall perennials. Their blues and whites give the garden a color pop. So relax and enjoy. Sure, there are gardening chores to do, but give yourself time to soak in the colors and celebrate the season.

Maples are a standout when it comes to foliage color. I grow many of the Japanese varieties, but I grow them in pots that I can move around to wherever I want added interest. Think of them as large bonsai. More fall color comes from the glowing yellow of *Ginkgo biloba* 'Princeton Sentry',

As the days grow cooler, we tend to spend more time closer to the house, appreciating the different hues and textures.

A Japanese maple in a plain terracotta pot close by the doorway, where I can appreciate the colors of its turning leaves and the various pumpkins and gourds beneath.

a fastigiate selection that is perfect for narrow beds, especially along a roadway. But the climbing *Hydrangea petiolaris* steals the spotlight: rivaling the color of a stained-glass window, the buttery yellow washes the entire wall of the barn. The *Polygonatum odoratum* 'Variegatum' that I use nearby also turns yellow in fall, and when backlit by the setting sun, it wonderfully echoes what is going on with the maples, ginkgo, and climbing hydrangea. The soft but bright yellow of *Amsonia hubrichtii* continues this color theme in the meadow and in the borders and containers. Herbaceous layer, shrub layer, and tree layer—all are evident here.

I'm in the second round of my love affair with *Rhus* (sumac), which has spectacular orange-yellow or orange-red fall color. I'm using these (non-poisonous) sumacs in the meadow and at the woodland's edge. Their appeal continues beyond fall, as their fuzzy, upright seed cones are not only attractive in the winter landscape but are also a food source for birds. Cotinus, well known for the feathery panicles that appear as a smoky haze in summer, also have splendid fall color. And *Berberis koreana*, which often gets a bad rap, turns a lovely red to orange in October. I use only *B. koreana* and its supposedly sterile forms; for me, it's slow to spread, without the invasive tendencies of some barberries.

Asters are a backbone of the fall flower garden, and they are a sparkling presence. *Aster tataricus* 'Jindai' is still blooming in late October and often blooms until frost. I use it in perennial borders and the meadow. It is shorter (at about 4 feet) than the straight species, vigorous, and stoloniferous (but easily divided); and its nectar-rich flowers, in shades of sky blue to lavender, are a magnet for migrating monarchs—I really like the idea that the flowers provide much-needed energy for them on their southward journey.

Most asters—including *Eurybia divaricata* whose whitish blooms cloud the woodland at this time of year—come with a bonus: they are deer resistant. Key word here is *resistant*, because a hungry deer will eat anything. Rabbits, however, sometimes eat the foliage of *Symphyotrichum oblongifolium* 'October Skies', which (along with *S. oblongifolium* 'Raydon's Favorite' and *S. laeve* 'Bluebird') is one of my favorite asters. I love the intensity of color in 'Bluebird', which was discovered as a seedling in a Connecticut garden and introduced by Richard Lighty of the Mt. Cuba Center.

Symphyotrichum cordifolium is in bloom in October, its various shades of blue like billowing clouds throughout the garden. This is a native aster that likes to sow about, and I allow it to do so, with minor control. The self-sown plants loosen up the design, but their masses of flowers contribute a certain unity to the garden through color repetition. They tie everything together, as the forget-me-nots do in spring. Gentians bring more blue to the fall garden. *Gentiana* 'True Blue' is easiest for me; I rely on it in pots and trough gardens, where I can control the soil pH. Gentians prefer acidic soil, and sulk or disappear in my only-slightly-acidic garden. When in doubt, use blue. You can't go wrong with it, as it goes with both hot and cool colors.

Actaeas provide a pop of white in the fall garden. They flower late, but they're worth waiting for. I like the bronze foliage color of *Actaea simplex* 'Brunette' and 'Black Negligee', which over the years have hybridized and spread, producing offspring in various shades of purple to purplish green. I also grow *A. simplex* 'White Pearl' and *A. racemosa*. I grow actaeas under my walnut trees (they withstand juglone), and I particularly like the tall flowering types. The 4-foot stems of creamy white flowers look like wands floating in the air above the autumn garden. They have a nice perfume as well, very light.

There are alternatives to chrysanthemums for fall display, and toad lilies (*Tricyrtis*) are my road less traveled. I gained an appreciation for these fall-flowering plants on trips to Japan. I think they are best used in narrow beds or along pathways, where the delicate beauty of their flowers stands a chance of catching the eye. I have them in the open garden and in pots, including a couple of weeping forms with yellow flowers in tall containers—an unexpected addition to the fall repertoire. Tricyrtis are not hard to grow in average to moist soil, although, like people, they can get stressed if conditions are not right. They spread steadily by stolons, or underground roots, to form colonies.

Dahlias have been blooming for months, but this is their last hurrah, as we usually have a frost in October. The vegetable garden is reduced to fall leaf crops and root crops, such as kale, collards, leeks, and beets. Tropicals and annuals like cosmos, fuchsias, and salvias are also enjoying

the last of their season. Salvias give me another wonderful shade of blue. I cut them as much as possible to beat the frost. Bulbs are still happening in October, including the first snowdrop, *Galanthus reginae-olgae*, discovered on a Greek mountain in 1876 and named for Queen Olga of Greece, the grandmother of Britain's Prince Philip. So, she was not only royal, she is an "immortal" to galanthophiles.

Opportunities for finding beauty in the October garden abound. It may be the shape of a seedpod, or something as fleeting as the silky seeds of milkweed floating in the air, or—a personal favorite of mine—rose hips. Hips come in a variety of shapes, colors, and sizes, and *Rosa* 'Geranium' produces some of the most dramatic. Its hips are long, orangey-apricot, and shaped like a perfume flacon. They are just as lovely as the simple flowers this rose produces in June. I appreciate all these things in the garden and in arrangements, especially in still-lifes. They remind me that after all, a flower, even a faded flower, retains its beauty in another form, and a seedpod holds the promise of a flower to come. In fact, I find the way a flower fades just as enticing as the bloom at its peak. Plants and gardens do not exist just in the moment of peak bloom but in a continuum of life. All stages are beautiful.

Berries I like include those of *Callicarpa* (beautyberry), whose brilliant fruit adds flash to the fall garden. I use both purple- and

white-berried callicarpas extensively in the garden and in arrangements—in fact, I grow them for arrangements as much as for the garden.

I use pumpkins, gourds, and acorns as seasonal accents in the garden. That may sound corny to some people, but you have to make the most of what you have in your quiver. I use whatever is available for compositions for my taborets. I think of them as playful creations that can be anything I want, with no limitations—unlike in other areas of the garden.

The color and drama of fall may bring the gardening season to a perfect crescendo, but there's still work to be done. There are bulbs to plant by the thousands. Leaves to rake and compost. Borders to cut back. And then there are the containers, hundreds of them, to be tucked inside for the winter, or moved to a less prominent spot if they are no longer a pleasing feature. This also helps keep the diminished garden from looking too busy. It's a constant, this editing of the garden.

In spring, it usually means adding pots and plants; in fall, more often it's taking away. Containers and plants, they all have to earn their keep. We only have so much space.

But comparing autumn to spring is like comparing Armagnac to Champagne—different, but both wonderful in their own right. I enjoy both.

The making of a meadowette

IT WAS THE LAST PIECE OF THE PUZZLE. The only part of the property that wasn't a garden. An irregular triangle edged on two sides by roads, it had been largely untouched except for mowing, and the addition of an oak tree given to me by a neighbor as a welcome gift almost three decades ago. There was also a single boulder, dropped off a truck by the developer of a nearby subdivision around the same time. As unlikely as it seemed, this scrap of hillside was destined to become a meadow. From a practical viewpoint, the driveway had become too small for all my visitors' cars, and it was completely overwhelmed with buses and cars on garden-tour days; now, visitors arriving by bus for tours would walk down through a meadow—a much more attractive introduction to the whole garden.

I had created meadows for many clients over the years, all on a much grander scale. This was to be a miniature meadow—a meadowette. The soil, if you could call it that, was terrible. The entire topsoil had been taken away, and the grade of the hill changed. My challenge was to put it back as it might have been. When we started, Michael picked up every little rock from this area and stored them in bulb crates. Now I'm bringing them all back, bit by bit, making little drifts of rocks.

A first step was to have more boulders placed by my friend Kai Pedersen, a talented landscape designer who studied in Japan. Placement is so important, and so permanent. It's not like, "Honey, can you move the sofa?" During my career, I have often seen the unfortunate placement of large stones ruin the look of a garden. We made sure ours were seated

properly—that is, partially buried in the ground, all striations going in
the same direction—and that the movement of each related to the other
stones. We wanted the meadow to look ancient yet contemporary, natural
yet ornamental, echoing that common gardening maxim, "Just enhance
nature." I followed the same ecological principles here as in the rest of the
garden: create habitats for birds and pollinators; right plant, right place. I
also wanted the meadow to peak at a different time from any of the other
gardens here at the cottage. Fall was my obvious choice.

We often think of meadows as purely herbaceous, and freeze them
in that time frame. I chose a more transitional time, as if the meadow had
been neglected for a few years and the woody plants had started to grow
in, just as they would in the wild. These woody plants also help to block
out unwanted views. All the plants for this space had to be extra tough, as

the conditions are inhospitable, so I continued to work with plants from my dry palette. The meadow grasses are short, largely warm-season growers that bloom in early fall. Our eastern meadows are often shorter than those in the Midwest. Eastern meadows are a result of our agricultural heritage, or they are clearings in the woods. They should look different from the tall grass meadows found in the Midwest. And they can be both ornamental and natural, as the two are not mutually exclusive.

There were several design considerations. First, the pitch of the slope itself had to be taken into account; that meant the steepness of the hill, and potential erosion once it was denuded. We had to plant it as fast as we could. Also, all my design angles changed. There was an abrupt edge where the meadow site meets the woods, and that transition needed to be softened. It was the perfect place for my beehives. They look like garden sentinels up on the hillside (think Easter Island), and after all the meadow was created for them, the pollinators. They even have their very own bee bath, a rock with a shallow depression that creates a pool. Bees need water, too. It's fun to see them crowding around the edge, quenching their thirst.

The soil was plain awful, but I decided not to amend it and instead stuck with my reliable mantra: respond to the site. Meadow plants prefer poor soils, because that is their natural environment. Getting them established is difficult, however, especially with no irrigation. We sprayed the hillside only once, to remove the weeds and crabgrass; otherwise, I rely on hand-weeding throughout the garden. I used a combination of plant sizes—gallons, quarts, and plugs. I like the idea of using different sizes for several reasons, cost being the first consideration. Varying the sizes makes the result look more natural, and positioning selected plants closer together can help to control weeds, too, depending on how fast the plants grow. The initial installation cost may be higher with larger sizes, but it is worth it in the long run because they fill in faster and minimize weed growth. Even so, the weeds won out the first couple of years.

Since the meadow is viewed from three sides, I had to consider those vantage points in planning the views and perspectives. The top of the meadow is an entrance to a subdivision that cannot be seen from below. I wanted to make that area more understandable to those who live in the subdivision, so I massed *Sesleria autumnalis* along the entry there. It looks more formal and is a suitable frame for the garden as well, giving it a different look on the north from the meadow below. Looking up from the driveway, I have a more naturalistic view—*Eragrostis spectabilis, E. elliottii, Sporobolus heterolepis.* These resemble a hazy mist when in

The idea was to have a succession-planting meadow—that is, woodies, grasses, and perennials showing the progression of the meadow's life.

Eragrostis spectabilis is common to most of my meadow designs.

bloom. Piercing through this mist are such grasses as *Schizachyrium scoparium* 'Standing Ovation' and *Andropogon gerardii* 'Blackhawks'. Most of the woody plants in my meadow have interesting fall color, and I used *Quercus robur* 'Purpurea' and other plants with purple foliage as accents. Even the sesleria and *Muhlenbergia capillaris* (pink muhly grass) go to rose instead of amber.

Never in my history with the garden have I altered the topography of the land. Here in my home garden, I wanted to respond to the earth as it was given to me. But on this hillside, in my meadow, I broke this rule. I gently scooped out a curvaceous pathway and contoured it down the slope. My hope was to create a path through the meadow that looked like it had been there forever, while making it easier for my guests, and me, to walk up and down the hillside. I also extended the existing stone wall from the lower garden halfway up the hill, tapering it so that it gradually disappears into the hillside. This part of the property now boasts more than 400 feet of hand-laid stone wall. It gives me pause that after almost 30 years, I am still building stone walls. Will I ever stop?

Although the meadow is intended to reach its peak in fall, the plants are chosen to make it appealing throughout the year. Woodies include many different cultivars and colors of *Ilex verticillata* (winterberry), which also allow for cutting, as well as *Quercus rugosa* and other scrub oaks from higher altitudes of the Southwest and Mexico to go along with the gift oak that was my original focal point. I also have the sumacs, which are common succession plants in meadows.

Perennials and bulbs are interplanted with the grasses. They are used sparingly, because this is a meadow, not a perennial border. I chose species bulbs and old-fashioned bulbs, shorter varieties so that I don't have to cut back the ripening foliage, which is hidden by the emerging grasses. The narcissus, whether species or antique, are white or pale yellow, offering a slightly different look from what I did in the woodland. I use *Galanthus elwesii* for naturalizing in this area; my fancy snowdrop cultivars are in the garden below. Camassias survived the winter, which surprised me (normally they like more moisture), so I am adding more.

Among the perennials, I grow *Liatris spicata* for June bloom, in addition to *L. microcephala* and *L. scariosa*. I love the *L. scariosa* as much as the monarchs do. One fall day I counted five on one plant. "Hurry up and drink," I tell them. "It's getting late in the season—time to go to Mexico!" Other perennials in the meadow include *Amsonia hubrichtii* for its fall color, *Eupatorium hyssopifolium*, *E. dubium* 'Baby Joe', and *Coreopsis integrifolia* 'Last Dance', which has personal connections for me. It was found at Sunny Border Nurseries, and we offered it to Mt. Cuba Center for its coreopsis trials, where it got high ratings. It blooms mid- to late October and grows only 2 to 3 feet tall. Mt. Cuba asked if I would like to name it, and we decided 'Last Dance' was apt. It gives us gardeners another plant to play with in October, pushing the limits of the growing season.

LEEK
(*or* ONION)
and CHEESE
TART

INGREDIENTS

3 to 4 tbsp olive oil
(or 3½ tbsp butter
if preferred)

6 mild sweet onions, chopped
(or 6 large leeks, washed,
dried, and thinly sliced)

Several sprigs of thyme,
tied with string

1 sheet ready-prepared
puff pastry, about 10 oz

¼ cup grated Parmesan
or shredded mozzarella

Salt and pepper

Alliums are an ancient plant. The Roman historian Herodotus recounted that inscriptions on the walls of the Pyramid of Cheops detail how much was spent on radishes, leeks, and onions for the workmen who built it around 2550 BC. Bread, raw onions, and beer was apparently a common midday meal for the poorer people of Egypt. Egyptians also offered alliums to the gods for a good harvest, but the priests who offered them were not allowed to eat them. Too bad! Many of the earlier forms of alliums used were edible, and they still are. We grow them in the vegetable garden—leeks, onions, chives, garlic—and use them liberally in cooking.

Michael made this tart with produce and herbs from our garden. Leeks are a little milder in taste, but you can use onions or a combination of the two.

METHOD

Preheat oven to 400 degrees Fahrenheit. Heat the oil or butter in a heavy-bottom saucepan and add the onions (or leeks) and thyme. Stirring as needed to prevent burning, slowly cook them until they are very soft and starting to caramelize. (Cover the pan initially to help them sweat, then remove it so that liquid evaporates.) Season with salt and pepper, and allow to cool. Meanwhile, place the puff pastry sheet on a lightly greased, nonstick baking sheet and bake for about 10 minutes, until it is puffed up and golden brown, and the bottom is cooked. Flatten the pastry by covering it evenly with the onion or leek mixture, leaving about ¼ inch around the edge. Sprinkle the cheese over the onion. Return to the oven for about 5 minutes to melt the cheese. Serve immediately.

opposite
Leek (or Onion) and Cheese Tart
makes a tasty lunch or brunch, or
can be paired with a tossed green
salad for an evening meal.

EASY
PICKLED
BEETS

INGREDIENTS

5 lbs beets, cooked,
   peeled, and cut into
   pieces of desired size

2 cups cider vinegar

½ cup water

2 cups sugar

1 tsp salt

½ to 1 tsp pepper

This easy recipe for pickled beets is from Michael's mother, Eva Alderfer. When Michael was growing up, beets were among the numerous fruits and vegetables his mother preserved, canned, or froze throughout the summer and autumn. Strawberries were turned into freezer jam, apples were made into sauce and frozen. She made sure she had enough bounty from the harvest to augment her family's meals throughout the winter.

These beets are so easy to make and good for you, too. If you don't grow your own beets, buy some fresh from a farmers' market to try this recipe.

METHOD

Sterilize the storage containers and lids.

Trim the tops from the beets, leaving about an inch of stem and roots to prevent the color from bleeding. Scrub the beets, then cook them in boiling water until just tender. Discard liquid. Cool the beets, trim off roots and stem, and peel. Cut into pieces of desired size.

Add all remaining ingredients to a large pot and bring to a boil. Add the cooked, chopped beets and heat thoroughly. Spoon into containers, seal tightly, and store in refrigerator for up to several months.

If preferred, can in jars according to the directions for your containers of choice.

opposite
Easy Pickled Beets, like any
pickled vegetables, are a wonderful
contribution to a healthy diet.

CHEESE PIE

INGREDIENTS

2 deep, 9-inch pie crusts

3 egg whites, beaten to
a stiff consistency

3 egg yolks, beaten

1 lb cottage cheese

8 oz cream cheese

¼ tsp salt

1¼ cups sugar

3 tbsp corn starch

1 large can evaporated milk

1¾ cups milk

If you like cheesecake, you are going to love this cheese pie. It is a Pennsylvania Dutch classic, a celebratory pie, meant to be eaten on special occasions. I consider it a just reward for a hard day of raking leaves.

I like this pie fresh-baked or cold. It can be served plain, or drizzled with dark molasses—which bumps it up a notch, in my opinion. This way of serving it is echt Deutsch, *or truly Pennsylvania Dutch. I don't know why people don't eat more molasses. They used to, and maybe it's coming back. Why not add a different flavor note? It works as an interesting counterpoint to the custard taste, and it also looks pretty.*

There are many versions of cheese pie. This recipe was passed on to us from Michael's mother, Eva Alderfer.

METHOD

Preheat oven to 450 degrees Fahrenheit. In a large bowl, cream the cottage cheese and the cream cheese. Add the egg yolks, salt, sugar, corn starch, evaporated milk, and milk, and mix until well blended. Fold the egg whites into the mixture, and pour into pie crusts.

Bake for 10 minutes at 450 degrees, then reduce heat to 350 degrees and bake for another 30 to 40 minutes.

opposite
Cheese Pie's only drawback is that
it disappears too quickly.

LATE
FALL

NOVEMBER

NOVEMBER HAPPENS TO BE one of my favorite months—but then, fellow gardeners, I have found a reason to love them all. If I had to describe November in a couple of words, they would be *leaves* and *bulbs*: this month can feel like a constant round of raking up leaves and planting bulbs. Well, almost constant. Especially at this time of year, I always make time for woodland walks, one of my great joys in life. I think of the woodland as my wider, wild garden. I like the smell of fallen leaves, the simple pleasure, since boyhood, of kicking them as I walk, the sound of them crackling beneath my feet. Some things you should never outgrow.

As I steal away for those walks in the woods or in my own garden, I respectfully glean objects for my winter wreaths or my decorative containers. By bringing them indoors, I find that these natural treasures help me to stay in touch with the outside world throughout the colder months. The key word here is *respectfully*, taking bits of nature's bounty but always leaving more than we take. Many of the objects of my affection are what most people think of as forest detritus—seeds, fallen branches, fungi. Whether hunting and gathering in our own woods or the larger forest, I walk with a backpack in which to bring my treasures home. Acorns, nuts, persimmons, holly berries, dried seedpods from milkweed or teasel, lichens, berries, mosses, Osage oranges fallen from trees that grow all over the place—whatever captures my imagination. I use all these things in my fall arrangements. But always the main thing is that I'm getting out, getting my inspiration from nature.

November is generally a month of big changes. If we have a warm fall, I may still be planting junipers or other woody plants if the soil is warm enough. This is a time when you can get some great deals at your

above
Some people may look at fall's leaves and see only the chore of their removal. I look at them and see art. These fall leaves, as arrangements on a taboret or tabletop, are my ode to fall. They may last only a day or two before they are blown away, but to me they speak of the color and brevity of the season, and how we should enjoy each moment in the garden.

opposite
Backlit leaves of *Cornus florida*, at once the obvious beauty of fall and the anticipation of spring. What I call "gardener's vision" is being able to see past, present, and future in one image.

The paths are raked, and the sun is even lower in the sky as we move from late fall into winter.

local garden center, because so many plants are on sale. But the weather can be tricky. A couple of years ago, we had no killing frost until mid-month. The leaves on some trees and shrubs—ginkgo, *Acer griseum*, corylopsis, edgeworthia—didn't change at all. They were freeze-dried on the trees. The paperbark maple looked like it was covered in white flowers. In all my years at Brandywine Cottage, I had never seen that happen. No matter how long you garden, each year is going to bring its own set of surprises and challenges. And I'm sure there will be something new next year.

That same fall, I planted four new dogwoods, *Cornus florida* 'Appalachian Spring', a selection that is resistant to anthracnose. Those trees have yet to mature. I'm not enamored with them in their juvenile state: they're too round. I hope they will, eventually, become more

natural-looking. Change happens with time in the garden, just as it does with us humans. I've never wanted the garden to be frozen in time, because gardening is an art form, and change is the essence of that living, growing, and dying art.

Bulbs dominate the planting schedule this month, many hundreds and hundreds of them. I don't think of this as a chore; rather, I think of it as paying forward for the joy I will receive come spring. I scatter the bulbs, dig a small hole, pop each bulb in, and offer a silent *Bless you, I hope to see you in the spring!*—which I usually do. Minor bulbs go in

above
Decay is part of fall. Instead of trying to hide it, why not call it what it is, and celebrate it? From left: peony seedpod; ornamental peppers; vegetable garden pepper.

above
Ginkgo biloba in fall color.

above right
When the leaves fall as they should, the papery bark of *Acer griseum* takes center stage.

first, in the rock garden, gravel garden, and meadow, as I have to plant perennials and grasses around them. Especially in the meadow, I planted the naturalizing bulbs first. Closer to the house, I use bulbs with not a lot of foliage—medium to short varieties, even the narcissus, so the leaves won't be a distraction in spring. We keep the design layer low so we don't get that eternal question: what do you do with the bulb foliage as it ripens? The answer is, you let it be. The bulbs need the nutrients produced through that foliage to develop flowers for next year.

In some ways, late fall offers a preview of spring. *Hamamelis virginiana* is decked out in its spidery pale yellow flowers, and *Galanthus elwesii* 'Barnes' and *G.* 'Potter's Prelude' are blooming. The very act of gardening causes us to look forward, to be optimistic. And the garden can be a very healing place. I can personally testify to that. Several times over the past couple of decades, I have been on the brink of death, and I credit the garden and its spirit with bringing me through. Often, all I

left
Cornus florida 'Appalachian Spring'
in fall color.

above
Maintenance doesn't take a break. A scene
often found by my front door—my favorite
gardening tools. With chores continuing, I
never want them far from reach.

November is for planting bulbs. Shown here are *Allium karataviense* bulbs in a hypertufa bowl, awaiting spring.

Hydrangea quercifolia. Almost any autumn leaf, when backlit, becomes as beautiful as a stained-glass window.

could do was sit in the garden and meditate. Gradually, I was able to start walking around the garden. When I started noticing the weeds, I knew I was on the way to recovery. The garden reinforced the idea that I am here for a purpose, as we all are. Nature wants to give back, if only we will let her. In my lifetime, I have seen rivers catch fire, but I've seen those same rivers come to life again, cleansed so that fish thrive once more. I have seen species pushed to the edge of extinction, yet recover. Eagles now fly over my backyard, and Peregrine falcons nest on city window sills—great examples of our species working with nature toward a return to Eden. Yes, I'm an optimist.

Once the planting and raking and cutting back are winding down, there's time in November to make use of the bounty we have gathered from the garden and the woods. Michael and I both work on

above
I often leave my spent hydrangea blossoms on the plant for interest, albeit a different kind of interest. I do remove them in early spring, so they won't detract from the fresh new growth.

these arrangements and holiday decorations, and we have the same philosophy—using the whole garden. Arrangements don't have to be about flowers; we use leaves and stems and pods and weeds. For indoor arrangements, foliage colors are beautiful on their own, or with a few flowers for highlights.

This is also when we pot up bulbs like amaryllis and paperwhites for indoor display over the next couple of months. In pots, bowls, and clear-glass vases and jars, the bulbs will bring a touch of the garden to side tables and window sills all over the house. Potting up paperwhites is a great way for beginner gardeners to gain confidence, and they make wonderful hostess gifts at this time of year, too. We always dress up our containers with sprigs of greenery or berries, or a top dressing of moss. It makes them look so much more festive.

This is a special month for me because it contains Thanksgiving, one of my favorite holidays. Although I try to be thankful every day, I like the idea of a specific time set aside for giving thanks. This is a holiday without much commercialism, one that requires only a heartfelt thank-you—for the gift of friendship, and for another year in the garden, living with plants. And almost always, it is the month in which we have our first fire in the hearth. It's that moment when you know you can sit back and take a deep breath. And then, refreshed, maybe even take another walk in the woods.

A miniature forest in a terrarium

above

A woodland scene Michael and I created. I've done terrariums that were meant to last, but this one was just for fun, to emulate the lushness of the forest floor—complete with quail eggs. We didn't bother looking for miniature plants, because I don't expect this to be forever.

above right

All our window sills easily accommodate our numerous collections of pots. I think you need indoor plants at this time of year, a reminder of the lushness of nature, to contrast with the snow that may soon be outside the window.

opposite

By late fall, not just our terrarium but almost all our houseplants, including this begonia, are inside.

PEOPLE WHO LIVED during the Victorian era may not have had laptops and Netflix to get them through the snowy winter months, but they did have their Wardian cases. These utilitarian wood-and-glass boxes were introduced early in Queen Victoria's reign to protect plants on long ocean voyages; once back on shore, in Britain and the United States, they evolved into ornate structures housing exotic ferns and orchids. I think they must have been a source of great pleasure for Victorians. And they still are, because Wardian cases are the direct fore-runners of our terrariums.

I like terrariums. They are great for winter months, another way to bring the outdoors in. The greenery cheers me on winter days and reminds me of my walks in the woods. And many are portable—you can move them from one place in the house to another, even if it's just for a dinner party. My terrarium is shaped like a large glass bottle set on its side, about 20 inches long and with tiny feet. I found it at the flea market my Quaker Meeting holds each fall; it was made to be a terrarium, a memento of the Philadelphia Bicentennial, which is stamped on its base, but it also "had my name on it."

Look around at flea markets or yard sales for interesting containers to house your own garden-in-glass, even if they aren't perfect. Gardening is often about found objects. Our terrarium was sold as a simple glass jar. Its glass is less than clear, probably to make it look more antique. But that aspect of the glass makes you want to—*look closer!* It's the mantra of late autumn, as it is for every other season of the year.

MIKE'S BUTTERNUT SQUASH RISOTTO
(vegetarian)

We both love risotto, and Mike adapted this recipe to take advantage of those vegetable garden stalwarts—butternut squash, spinach, and thyme. Most squash are excellent storage vegetables, too, and butternut squash should last for a few months if properly stored. Don't remove the squash from the vine until it's fully ripe, usually by early October, to allow the skin to thicken properly. Store in a cool, dark space with low humidity.

This recipe makes an excellent vegetarian meal or side dish. Experiment by adding or substituting other produce from your vegetable garden, such as diced red pepper, zucchini, asparagus, or broccoli.

INGREDIENTS

1 butternut squash, about 2½ lbs, peeled, cleaned, and cut into 1-inch dice

4 tbsp olive oil

3 shallots, minced

1 tbsp fresh thyme, chopped

¼ cup dry white wine

2 cups arborio rice

4½ cups vegetable stock

3 very large portobella mushrooms, diced

1 cup baby spinach leaves, stems removed

¾ cup Parmesan

Salt and pepper to taste

METHOD

In a heavy pot, heat 2 tbsp olive oil and add the diced butternut squash. Cook on medium heat for 5 to 10 minutes, until it starts to soften. Remove from heat and transfer to a bowl. Set aside.

Add 1 tbsp of the remaining olive oil to the heavy pot, add minced shallots and thyme and sauté over medium heat for 5 minutes. Add the wine and rice. Stir for about a minute, then start adding the vegetable stock half a cup at a time, stirring constantly. Add stock until you have a nice, creamy consistency. Add butternut squash and stir.

In a separate pan, sauté diced portobella mushrooms in remaining olive oil for 5 to 10 minutes, then add to rice mixture. Add the Parmesan and stir well. Continue cooking for another 15 minutes until creamy. Add baby spinach leaves and continue stirring until spinach wilts and all ingredients are well combined, adding vegetable broth as needed. Season with salt and pepper to taste. Serve immediately, with a garnish of thyme sprig or baby spinach leaf on each plate as desired. Serve as a vegetarian main course, or, for non-vegetarians, as a side dish with turkey, lamb, or other meat of choice.

opposite
Mike's Butternut Squash Risotto is wonderful comfort food, especially on a chilly late fall day.

NAVY BEAN
PIE

INGREDIENTS

9-inch pie crust

2 eggs, lightly beaten

1 cup evaporated milk

2 cups cooked and
   mashed navy beans

¾ cup sugar

1 tsp cinnamon

1 tsp nutmeg

1 tsp vanilla extract

½ tsp salt

½ tsp ginger

½ tsp clove

Navy Bean Pie is part of American history. It's also nutritious and delicious, and when I was a kid, it was a favorite alternative to pumpkin pie. An African-American woman who helped my mother out with cooking from time to time introduced my family to Navy Bean Pie. Whenever it was served to guests, it was a huge hit and a conversation piece. But culturally it was more than a dessert. Navy Bean Pie grew out of the efforts of African-American Muslims in the 1930s to establish an identity that was independent of the legacy of slavery. This bean pie was made to replace sweet potato pie.

Navy beans are easy to grow, like bush beans, and very high in protein; harvest the beans when they ripen in summer, and dry them in a single layer on a counter until they harden. If you aren't growing them this year, you can use canned or dry navy beans from the store. Before cooking with dry beans, soak them overnight.

This recipe is the bean pie I grew up with. Serve it plain, or with whipped cream.

METHOD

Preheat oven to 425 degrees Fahrenheit. In a large bowl, combine eggs and evaporated milk, and stir. Add beans, sugar, salt, vanilla, and all spices, and beat with a mixer at low speed until well blended. Pour the mixture into the pie crust.

Bake for 15 minutes at 425 degrees, then reduce heat to 350 degrees and bake for another 35 minutes, or until a knife inserted in the center of the pie comes out clean. Serve warm or cold, with whipped cream if desired.

opposite
Navy Bean Pie naturally speaks of
fall to me.

WINTER

DECEMBER

THE WINTER HOLIDAYS are all about bringing light to darkness. Often, this is viewed in a spiritual or sacred way, but whether it's a Christian concept, or a festival of lights, or a winter solstice celebration—one way or another, they center on light. And the short days of December offer us plenty of opportunities for a literal interpretation of bringing light to darkness.

We create as much light as we can at the cottage. Christmas lights are strung not only on the tree inside but along the porch roofline and outlining exterior doors and windows. Oil lanterns adorn the porch and the picnic table, a fire burns in the stove within the hearth, and we place candles everywhere, indoors and out. Many candles are clustered with pine cones and greenery atop the covered well, giving a welcoming glow to the entryway.

opposite
My traditional holiday wreath. It is covered with nuts, fungi, lichens, red ilex berries, various pods and pine cones, and pheasant feathers

right
Atop the wood box on the porch is a red railroad oil lantern that we use as a Christmas light. Michael's uncle, Norm Rittenhouse, collected lanterns such as this one from the Pennsylvania Railroad.

far right
The covered well, this time ornamented with candles in glass jars surrounded by sprays of incense cedar.

above
It's not just the first bonfire,
but the opportunity to roast
marshmallows.

opposite
A crock full of *Ilex verticillata*
branches, flanked by two redware
flowerpots topped with moss.

But the most dramatic light may come from our bonfires—a winter bonus. All the elements in the garden are important to me, and that includes fire. We light a bonfire for as many winter occasions and holidays as possible, building it from garden trimmings and fallen branches. It certainly makes the chore of picking up sticks more fun. Into the fire they go, and later some of the ash will go into the compost and eventually back into the garden.

Gardeners are acutely aware of the rhythms of light and dark, which are so important to plants. But even if much of the outside world retreats in the cold weather, winter is not a dead season in your garden. It's just that you are called upon to view it in a different way. Start by looking at the structure—the bones of the garden. This is the time to see and appreciate different aspects of it. In winter, when plants aren't

Winter bonfires have their own special warmth and are especially celebratory on Solstice. We light ours in the northwest corner of the garden, with a bench and chair made from woven willow set around it.

covered with leaves, we learn to value their branching, the beautiful bark, and their general shape. I can appreciate the bare forms of deciduous trees outlined against the evergreens and especially the sky, their silhouettes a contrast of darkness and light. The sun is lower in the sky, not directly overhead as it is in summer, so the light is less intense and creates interesting shadows. The color read is different, and snow or ice adds a little crispness.

In addition to being an effective insulator, snow excels as a natural decorator. A lacy dusting on the top of a Cinderella pumpkin makes the heirloom vegetable look like a fitting coach for that fairytale princess, and snow patterns on the hellebore leaves turn the hellebore border into a dazzling design that is visible from the cottage windows (that's why we don't start cutting them back until after the new year). *Rohdea japonica* looks appealing with a dusting of snow as well; it gives you a vertical evergreen shape in winter, which is really useful. Varying your textures makes a garden look more interesting.

I get a lot of pleasure in the winter garden just from the bonfires and from the little vignettes I continue to create on the taborets, using seasonal fruits like cranberries and persimmons, or oranges, that traditional Christmas symbol of charity. So my enjoyment of my garden doesn't depend on plants in bloom—but I demand that as well.

above
On this taboret, a bowl full
of cranberries topped with
persimmons, nestled in greenery.

above right
A taboret featuring oranges and
white pine.

opposite
Even pumpkins that have survived
the frost take on a different
persona with snow.

I try to have something in bloom every day, as challenging as that is. What is usually flowering in December? Some hellebores on the hillside, the fall-blooming crocus at the end of the drive; and I have snowdrops that bloom all winter, so I know all is not lost! The mahonias have budded up, and the edgeworthias are covered in elegant little bell-like buds. Foliage adds a colorful note. I think the chief beauty of *Leucothoe axillaris* is its winter color, a beautiful deep burgundy on the hillside. I like leucothoe with the yellow textural contrast of *Cephalotaxus harringtonia* 'Golden Dragon', which provides a vertical element and is deer resistant. Deer will eat yew but not this false yew. *Cryptomeria japonica* also has lovely texture and beautiful foliage that is perfect for Christmas greens; we have four different selections of it. Many Shinto shrines in Japan are built with its wood; so are the chopsticks I bought for myself in Japan.

For a time in December, I can look out my kitchen window and see bluebirds feeding on *Ilex verticillata* berries. They eat the red ones first.

Even if the berries last only a fleeting time, it's worth it just for that sight. And the birds need the food in the cold. We must never forget, we aren't gardening only for ourselves; we have to be cognizant of our role in the greater garden—the earth and its plants and creatures—of which we are a part. We put more red winterberries in the window box on the porch, with Osage oranges, magnolia leaves, and other greenery. Tucked in among them we nestle pots of white-flowering *Helleborus niger* (Christmas rose). It is lovely to be able to look through the kitchen window and see white flowers outside, complementing the white snow. Hellebores can take frost and cold, but if temperatures in the low 20s are forecast, it's easy to pull the pots out of the window box and put them in the barn.

Magnolia leaves are useful in many holiday displays. *Magnolia grandiflora* 'Edith Bogue', the first selection of that species found to be hardy in the Philadelphia area, has glossy, dark green leaves with pretty grayish brown undersides. I have grown it for about 20 years, alongside

above
Euphorbia ×martini 'Ascot
Rainbow' underplanted with
acorus in a terracotta pot—made
200 percent better with cut
branches of *Magnolia grandiflora*
and red ilex berries.

the native *M. virginiana*. Sometimes I make wreaths with its leaves reversed, or I mix it up and do some green, some brown. For a different effect, I might combine magnolia leaves with juniper berries in a green and blue display. We dress up many of our outdoor containers with berries, greenery, and colorful foliage. How hard is it to stick a few pieces of evergreen in a pot? It makes it look 200 percent better. In December, the rock garden has been changed over to evergreens and winter containers, too. Hardier plants like callicarpa or amsonia are featured in smaller pots, so that I can take them out and put them in the garden later. My great hope for the garden is that every time you walk through, you see something you didn't see before.

Of course, we never know what winter will bring, or how cold it will get, but we have to be prepared. Climate change has brought with it extreme swings of temperature and increasingly dramatic weather. Our winters may be very warm, or very cold. We think we have a warm zone 7 garden here in the mid-Atlantic, but suddenly we are back in zone 6. It's the fluctuations that hurt the plants. Because I have winter shelter in my barn and on my many wide window sills, I am free to test the limits when it comes to acquiring tender or borderline-tender plants. Most gardeners have zonal envy—and at least a few plants that enjoy temperatures a half-zone or warmer than the one in which they garden. But in a winter like some we've had recently, you pay. Try to avoid acquiring vulnerable plants if you can't protect them or bring them in. When temperatures plunge, I worry about my *Mahonia eurybracteata* subsp. *ganpinensis* 'Soft Caress' (I have put a box over it when temperatures dropped below 10 degrees) or whether the edgeworthias need protection. So far, they haven't, but it's always a gamble.

Gardeners have to make a decision about how much they are willing to do to grow what they want. If a plant means a lot to you, you take care of it. Having spent a lot of time in the South, I am attached to camellias, and so I do what it takes to accommodate their needs, including hauling them in and out of shelter, so that I can enjoy them. I don't like putting boxes over everything to protect the plants; it makes the garden look like a trash truck exploded. But I have many glass cloches! They are decorative and reflect the light, but they are also useful. I do group some of my more-tender plants together in a protected spot, and in the nursery area I cover some up with a tarp. One year, when I was younger and more ambitious, I dug holes and put pots-and-all into the ground. I have tried just about everything at one time or another. There are so many plants; I wish I had more time so that I could bring more inside. I describe myself as a horticultural acrobat, but there's never enough time—whether it's gathering flowers or putting plants away for winter.

The plants aren't the only living things that may need winter shelter. If it gets really cold, we trundle our chickens into the barn to protect them, and keep them in there for the duration of the frigid weather. Just as with plants, it's good to keep the chickens acclimated to the weather, within reason. If you let them outdoors in really frigid temperatures, however, their combs can freeze.

Winter gives you an opportunity to read your landscape. I'm out on my hillside after a snowfall, looking for where the snow melts first, as that is where I can put something that is borderline hardy. People say plants don't talk, but they do—they tell you what they want all the time. Look for the spots that hold moisture after it rains, for example. You just have to be observant.

Inevitably, some plants won't survive an abnormally cold winter. At the close of one of my lectures, I ask my students what beauty is. Part of my answer? *Beauty is compassion.* Having compassion for a plant or a chicken is a good thing—there are certain plants that need a little extra help. I try not to have too many like that, but when you grow more than 3,000 plants, there are a few that fall off the bell curve. I usually tell my students not to take these losses personally, that I've probably killed more plants than all of them combined, because I've been at it a long time. On the up side, every loss provides an opportunity to buy something else. However, it's sad when you lose a treasured plant. A plant that was given to you by a dear friend, even if it is the most common plant, is a cherished plant. There is an emotional connection to the garden that is the soul of the garden. When I walk through my garden I don't just see plants—I see people and places and moments. Those are layers of emotional attachment, and they are just as real as the actual plants.

O, Christmas tree!

MICHAEL AND I BOTH LOVE CHRISTMAS. There is a rhythm to the seasons, and cutting our own Christmas tree is part of the rhythm of our winter. If the holidays are all about tradition, and they are, then cutting and decorating the tree is as much a tradition of this season as having a fire.

My Grandfather Thorpe used to cut a tree from the family farm when I was a boy. Now, on the day after Thanksgiving every year, Michael and I go out to a Chester County farm and cut our tree. We put it up immediately, placing it in water in an old-fashioned tree stand, but for a while we just look at it in the green. Next, Michael begins stringing the lights on the tree, hundreds of lights, not just on the tips of the branches but woven all through the tree to show off its structure and to give it depth. At this stage, my role is generally to urge, "It needs more!" By the time we're through, there could be as many as a thousand lights illuminating its branches, depending on the size of the tree.

Finally, we start adding the ornaments, about a thousand of them, though again it depends on the tree's size. We often laugh that we need a strong tree to support them. They are all blown glass, in the German tradition—and in the tradition of the Culp family. A couple were handed down from my Grandmother Culp, antique glass balls that have faded to a lovely patina. And I started collecting ornaments many years ago, when I had my first house. We buy them to commemorate events, or as vacation souvenirs. Now I've started giving an ornament each year to my nieces, so the tradition continues.

I like to hang the larger ornaments all over the tree first, placing them, like the strings of lights, deep within the branches as well as on the outer extremities to give the tree dimension and depth. Next come the strings of beads. Because they are glass, we can't put them on last and risk breaking the other glass ornaments. But no matter how careful we are, at least one ornament is broken—which is why I buy another one or two every year. The smaller, lighter ornaments go on last, once again positioned throughout the tree.

Numerous though they are, almost every one of the hundreds of ornaments has special meaning. Of course there's a bulldog ornament—or three. And many years ago my two younger sisters jokingly presented me with a family of glass sheep, two white ... and one black. Some ornaments

above
Outdoors, on a taboret, I sometimes create a miniature echo of our Christmas tree by adorning a potted tree with tiny ornaments. Yes, it does resemble Charlie Brown's tree, but I love it just as much as the big indoor one. I usually handle the decorations on this one myself.

bear a more serious weight of tradition, carried here from Germany. One that was special to children in Germany is the green pickle. According to folklore, the pickle was the last ornament hung when the tree was decorated on Christmas Eve. The following morning, the first child to find the pickle received an extra present—ostensibly left by St. Nicholas as a reward for being observant. Now there's a man who'd like my gardening mantra: *Look closer!*

The most unlikely ornament tied to Christmas revelry may be Krampus, a folkloric figure who in centuries past accompanied St. Nicholas in parts of Germany and Austria. The devilish Krampus punished children who had misbehaved, in contrast to St. Nick, who

above
Everything on the tree has special meaning, the story of our lives told through ornaments: a white sheep; the green pickle; Krampus.

opposite
Not just a day but a season—for us, it's all about celebrating light. A live tree featuring traditional German glass ornaments and hundreds of tiny lights is the focal point of our dining room throughout winter.

rewarded good boys and girls with sweets. Until the last decade or so, Krampus was virtually unknown in the United States, but several recent holiday horror films have turned him into quite a popular character.

Overall, we take our Christmas down the same way we put it up—gradually. The red bows come off first, and the greenery is removed as it starts looking tired. We leave our tree up well into January, because it brings light into the darkest part of the year. And it's such a lot of work! We want to enjoy it. The last things to come down are the roping and the wreaths on the porch, because my outdoor wreaths are as much about winter as Christmas. Finally, all that's left is the wreath between the doors, this past year an elegant concoction that, as always, included things gathered on our earlier walks in the woods.

ROASTED VEGETABLE "TWO-FER"

INGREDIENTS

Enough carrots, sweet
potatoes, butternut squash,
parsnips, white potatoes,
celeriac root, beets (or
any other vegetable you
like) for two meals

Olive oil

Salt and other preferred
seasonings, such as black
pepper, rosemary, or thyme

Chicken or vegetable
stock for the soup

*Root vegetables and chilly weather seem made for each other. Roasted
with any other vegetables of your choice, they are a favorite side dish for
Thanksgiving and Christmas dinners and other festive meals, but roasted
vegetables can make almost any meal feel quite special.*

*Michael likes roasted vegetables served with a roasted chicken. But, he
points out, with a little extra effort you can prepare two quite different
meals simultaneously—roasted vegetables with your meat of choice and
roasted vegetable soup. Both are delicious.*

*If you choose to use beets, he suggests oiling and cooking them separately,
as they tend to bleed and turn the other vegetables red.*

METHOD

Preheat oven to 400 degrees Fahrenheit. Line several roasting pans or
rimmed cookie sheets with parchment.

Scrub and/or peel the vegetables, and cut into pieces of similar size. In
a large bowl, stir together oil and salt, plus any other seasonings you
choose. Toss the vegetable pieces in the oil to coat evenly.

Distribute the vegetables in a single layer on the parchment-lined pans,
with the beets on a pan by themselves. Roast in the oven for about 45 minutes, or until fork-tender and browned.

Serve half the vegetables immediately, and refrigerate the rest for a day
or two until you are ready to make soup.

opposite
Roasted Vegetable "Two-Fer."
One batch of roasted vegetables
makes a delicious accompaniment
to a baked dinner. Do a second
batch at the same time as the
base for another meal, Roasted
Vegetable Soup.

ROASTED VEGETABLE SOUP

Add the roasted vegetables and any other leftover vegetables to a pot and puree them with an immersion blender, if you have one; or puree the vegetables in an ordinary blender and transfer to a saucepan.

Over medium heat, slowly add chicken or vegetable stock, stirring constantly, until the soup reaches the desired consistency. Heat thoroughly. Ladle into serving bowls and serve immediately, topped with croutons if desired.

opposite
Roasted Vegetable Soup is the second meal from Michael's Roasted Vegetable "Two-Fer."

PERSIMMON PUDDING

INGREDIENTS

About 4 large or 6 small ripe persimmons—enough to make about 2 cups of pulp

3 eggs

1¼ cups sugar

1 to 1½ cups all-purpose flour (depending on type of fruit used)

1 tsp baking powder

1 tsp baking soda

½ tsp salt

½ cup melted butter

2½ cups whole milk

2 tsp cinnamon

1 tsp ginger

½ tsp freshly grated nutmeg

1 cup of raisins *or* nut meats (optional)

Persimmons are an underrated fall fruit that should be on the menu much more often. The most widely grown persimmon is the Asian or Japanese variety, Diospyros kaki, *which produces fruits about the size of a peach. But this pudding can also be made using the smaller fruit of the native persimmon,* D. virginiana, *hardy in zones 4 through 9. The fruits need to be soft and ripe, or they will taste too tart. The Japanese variety is very juicy, and will require a little more flour in this recipe; the native fruit may give a slightly waxy consistency to the pudding.*

I don't grow persimmons, but there is a tree within sight of the Meeting House I attend. Both the native and the Japanese trees put on a colorful display in fall, and the orange fruits are attractive, too. Team them up with bright red cranberries and a bit of seasonal greenery for a great outdoor display in late fall, then take them indoors to make persimmon pudding, if some varmint hasn't gotten to them!

There are many versions of puddings using persimmons. This recipe was passed along to us by Elise du Pont.

METHOD

Preheat oven to 325 degrees Fahrenheit.

Cut the tops from the persimmons and scoop out the soft fruit with a spoon. Force it through a sieve or colander to yield about 2 cups of pulp in a bowl. Beat in the eggs, sugar, flour (adjusting for the juiciness of the fruit), baking powder, baking soda, salt, melted butter, milk, cinnamon, ginger, and nutmeg. If desired, stir a cup of raisins or nut meats into the batter.

Pour the batter into a greased 9-by-9-inch baking dish. Bake until firm, about 1 hour. Serve with cream or hard sauce.

opposite
Persimmon Pudding is a classic Southern dessert.

JANUARY

JANUARY, A TIME FOR DREAMING of things to come, of planning for the future. No one can say that this month is the best time for gardening, yet I have done some of my best gardening in it. We all expect ice, cold rain, snow at this time of year, but there are always warmer days when you can get out and enjoy a hint of spring.

What draws us to the garden in winter? Perhaps it has something to do with chlorophyll withdrawal. Or maybe I still garden on Southern time, since I spent so many years creating gardens in Georgia and North Carolina before moving back to Pennsylvania, where I grew up. But I like the idea that it alters our sense of time and perspective. I've often felt the garden in winter is like Renaissance art, where the effect of light on nature comes into sharp focus; or like the church in Lent, where everything is stripped to essentials. In January, the garden's glorious bones are exposed. Now is the time to appreciate beautiful bark, how the angle of the sun affects colors, how light bounces off frozen water.

But there is color in winter. Although hamamelis may not be at peak bloom in January, they begin to show colors then—a time of the

top row
Winter can be thought of in two ways: as a time for color or as a time for restraint in your palette. From left, some variations on the latter: *Crataegus monogyna* bark; *Hakonechloa macra* 'Aureola'; *Chasmanthium latifolium* seedheads.

above
Dwarf sedum in hollowed-log container.

above right
Containers in combination in the winter garden.

year when we need this: as much as I like snowdrops and hellebores, the winter garden should not be built around one or two plants. The plants that bloom at this time of year, like an orange-flowered witchhazel, hold a special place in my heart. These are plants with spirit, and though they may not appear in numbers, their scarcity allows me to study each flower more closely and marvel at its detail. In January I have the luxury of time—no gardener can do this in June!

The earliest snowdrops continue to appear in January, and excitement starts to build as the tiny white buds, protected by their spathe, emerge from the earth. The leaves have hardened tips that allow them to push through frozen soil, and their sap contains a kind of antifreeze. It still amazes me how fast they grow in just one warm day.

Galanthus tucked in under a blanket of snow. Galanthophile challenge! Can you name the colors of the markings on these snowdrops, even when not in bloom—or in sight, for that matter?

Some gardeners put their winter gardens close to the house, so they can enjoy what the season has to offer without braving the cold. But I also like to plant far away, so that I am forced to venture out to discover what's happening. Walking into the garden to admire the red berries of an aucuba gets me outside, where I love to be. It's good for your health! It's also good for the plants. Walking around, I can do simple tasks like removing the old leaves from the hellebores before the flower buds emerge, or cutting the leaves off the witchhazels so you can see the blooms better. I don't obsess over these chores; I just do a bit every day. And while I am doing this, I can look more closely at the blossoms themselves, so it's not really work.

You really can see what is going on in the garden as you walk around doing these chores, and there are unexpected rewards. One winter day,

above

Aucuba japonica 'Variegata' is hardy in zones 6 through 9. In winter months, bright berries and evergreen foliage become very important.

above right

Here, the yellow variegation of the aucuba leaves stands out amid euphorbia, ghost bramble, and magnolia branches. This time, the red berries are courtesy of *Ilex verticillata*.

thinking ahead to that Sunday's arrangement for the Quaker Meeting, I feared there would not be much available to work with in the garden. But by bundling up and walking around it, I was able to gather orange *Ilex verticillata* berries, silvery edgeworthia buds, green *Helleborus foetidus* flowers, and pale yellow berries from *Nandina domestica* var. *leucocarpa*. I added some dried hydrangeas that I had left on the plants from the previous summer, and the whole effect was rather delicate and ethereal—perfect for Meeting.

The taborets are more apparent in winter, too. One might highlight pine cones and decorative stones. Another could feature a clear crystal glass of water reflecting a seashell and a hellebore flower laid next to it. Sometimes I place an arrangement directly on the stone, sometimes in water, or I may change the display as I walk by—it depends on my mood and my whim. Sometimes artist friends move things around. I like it

Add a welcome touch of color to the winter garden with *Ilex verticillata* berries. From left: 'Winter Gold'; 'Afterglow'; 'Winter Red'.

Almost anything can become an objet d'art in the garden, if it is pleasing to you, and all take on a different dimension when dusted with snow. From left: Wave Hill chairs; birdhouse by a local ceramic artist; French terracotta olive jar.

when artists from different disciplines interact. It's all ephemeral, which speaks to me of the nature of the garden, but it should be joyful, because the beauty comes out of that joy.

I enjoy connecting with nature 12 months of the year, and year-round gardening enriches the experience. Snow or frost add another dimension. Even tasks like sharpening tools and repairing stone walls allow me to connect. Working on our stone wall is definitely a winter job, because we don't have the luxury of time in the warmer months. Repair is always necessary, as the wall is laid without mortar. It looks more natural and goes with the style of the house. Natural stone is one of the unifying elements of the garden, from the wall to pathways, borders, taborets, even random stones placed as accents. Mike and I built the wall ourselves, and it is one of my pet projects. Because I have been working on it for 27 years, I often feel like an ancient Egyptian, endlessly building the pyramids. I still add stones—a few here, a few there. The wall, like the garden, is never done.

No, January is not a dull month. It is merely different, a time of hope and promise, when the days are getting longer and the year and the garden are beginning another cycle.

opposite
Potted *Schizachyrium scoparium* 'Standing Ovation' and ornamental cabbage, dressed up with ilex berries and cut branches of magnolia and cryptomeria.

Celebrating the new year

ON NEW YEAR'S DAY we sometimes have friends over to celebrate, and in fine weather we gather around a huge bonfire to toast the new year in Champagne. How rare to be able to do that outdoors! On one recent New Year's, we took our guests on a garden walk to see what was flowering on this first day of the new year. Everyone admired a black double hellebore in full bloom, one of the Brandywine hybrids, and *Galanthus plicatus* 'Three Ships' was still in flower. This little snowdrop got its name because it always seems to bloom for Christmas Day, which is rare for a plicatus. It owes its name to that old English Christmas carol: "I saw three ships come sailing in / On Christmas Day, on Christmas Day; / I saw three ships come sailing in / On Christmas Day in the morning." But this snowdrop, with its unusually early bright white flowers, almost didn't survive to grow in our gardens. Galanthophile John Morley found it in 1984, growing under an ancient cork oak in a pasture in Henham Park in southern England. He dug some of it up and passed it around, which was a very good thing, as park cattle later trampled the patch, wiping out the colony. This snowdrop now exists only in cultivation, but it's a vigorous grower and reliably blooms for the holidays.

above
You can begin to anticipate the coming seasons by the bud set of certain plants, as seen here with *Edgeworthia chrysantha*.

left
The meadowette in its first winter.

Aside from my diehard galanthophile friends, however, it was the unusual buds of *Edgeworthia chrysantha* that drew the most comments from garden guests. The silky, silvery buds of this mid-size shrub are beautiful, and when the buds open into yellow flowers a couple of months later, they have an unusual but appealing fragrance.

Two more edgeworthias followed me home from a plant show shortly after this garden walk. Plant shows offer a different kind of plant hunting. I actually did need those edgeworthias for my hillside, but there were also some cryptomerias and juniper I had to have, too, because, well, plant lust. They are welcome additions to the winter garden. I always have plants that I haven't yet found homes for, but never do I have regrets about acquiring them. There is something soulless about limiting yourself to a list and not buying a plant you love. A good garden artist can make it work.

After our walk in the winter garden, it was time to move indoors to enjoy another gift from the garden—homemade sauerkraut, featuring cabbages from the fall harvest, paired with richly flavorful pork: a traditional Pennsylvania Dutch feast to welcome a new year.

opposite
Lindera glauca var. *salicifolia* is a favorite here at the cottage: beautiful fall color, black berries, and foliage that fades to taupe in winter, blending nicely with the meadow grasses.

Winter gardens: a vivarium in the basement

ORIGINALLY, THE BASEMENT at Brandywine Cottage, which probably had been used as a root cellar, could be accessed only by a set of stairs that led up to the outdoor porch. The old stone steps are beautiful, and I thought I could use them to make this subterranean living area less like a basement by displaying potted plants on them.

After a year of using grow lights, I had an epiphany—the stairwell could act as a skylight. If we got rid of the heavy wooden cellar doors, not only would we have a view of the outside world during the winter months, we could bring some of the garden indoors. French doors on the exterior entryway let the light in, and sliding glass doors at the base allow us to keep the temperature between 40 and 50 degrees. I augment the natural light with grow lights alternated with fluorescent lights, for a more varied range.

For the last few years, this has been the winter home for a variety of potted plants—*Fatsia japonica*, tender ferns, orchids, cycads, kniphofias, a few pelargoniums to give a color note. But primarily it is the winter staging ground for much of my clivia collection. I have clivias from all over the world, including a *Clivia gardenii* from South Africa that I bid on at a Longwood Rare Plant Auction at least 15 years ago. I like the

straight species because it blooms at an off time, around Thanksgiving, with very elegant tubular flowers that are orange with green tips. I also have variegated clivias and other rare leaf forms from China and four different cultivars of the yellow form. One of them I acquired more than 20 years ago, when I was visiting Charles Cresson, a consummate plantsman who was a major influence in my gardening life. When I admired his yellow clivia, Charles offered to give me a seed. I planted it, and it germinated the following year, but it took several more years to bloom. That

was my first yellow clivia, and I treasure it because I got it from Charles. I was growing it before I got one from Sir John Thouron, who grew the rare yellow clivia at Doe Run, his property in the Brandywine Valley. Sir John's yellow is still prized for its distinguished lineage—and you can always spot it because the plant grows in a vase shape. It's different from other yellows.

In the middle of the plants sits a Tibetan Buddha that I found at Rehoboth Beach. The minute I saw it I knew it would be perfect for the stairwell. Where there had been nothing but plants, this little figure would provide focus and add a spiritual dimension. Sometime later I acquired a string of Tibetan prayer flags, and I hung them in with the plants, too. Almost everything in the open garden is utilitarian. This display is a bit whimsical, but because this space is fairly isolated from the rest of the house, I decided I could do something a little different, as long as it wasn't overly kitschy. You have to allow for some spontaneity in the garden, something that makes the garden yours, or it risks becoming gardening-by-numbers. If something speaks to you, try to find a place to use it. I don't do everything right; I do want to empower people to do what they love.

above
Variegated Chinese clivia. I grow it for its foliage; the flower is a bonus.

above right
The Tibetan Buddha seems quite at home among clivias and orchids.

opposite
We turned the steps down to the basement into a vivarium, illuminated by both natural and artificial light. It makes the basement seem less like a basement and more like a greenhouse.

DAVID'S HOMEMADE SAUERKRAUT

INGREDIENTS

20 to 25 lbs of cabbage
(2 medium heads
equal about 5 lbs)

1 cup kosher salt;
more as needed

Large crock or container,
glass or enamel-coated
(around 5 gallons;
sometimes I use a 4-gallon
crock, which accommodates
about 20 lbs of cabbage)

2 large plastic freezer bags
(preferably 2-gallon size);
old-timers used a stone
on top of a plate to weigh
down fermenting cabbage

In the Pennsylvania Dutch region of Pennsylvania, New Year's Day wouldn't be complete without a feast of pork and sauerkraut. Both Mike and I grew up with this tradition. I've watched people making kraut all my life—it was just something everyone did. Mike's father and grandfather had stands at Philadelphia's Reading Terminal Market, selling products (including sauerkraut) from their farm. Today, naturally fermented foods are widely—even wildly—popular again, and some research suggests that the beneficial bacteria found in fermented foods like sauerkraut strengthen our gut health by increasing the number of healthy probiotics.

But why is it associated with New Year's Day? Folklore, probably. Eating sauerkraut was traditionally believed to bring blessings and prosperity for the year ahead. Some old New Year toasts suggest that the more long strips of cabbage you have in your crockpot, the more luck and money you will enjoy through the year. I always make my own sauerkraut with cabbage from the kitchen garden to serve with pork on New Year's Day. Not only do I have a collection of antique crocks in which to ferment the cabbage, but my coffee table is an antique cabbage shredder.

Here is my recipe, with step-by-step instructions. You can adjust it up or down, to fill gallon jars or smaller containers—just make sure to use 4 tablespoons of kosher salt for every 5 pounds of cabbage.

METHOD

1. Sanitize crock and utensils.

2. Remove outer leaves and cores of cabbage.

3. Slice cabbage into thin strips.

4. As you slice, mix 4 tbsp salt with every 5 lbs of cabbage; let stand in a large bowl to wilt a little. (Do *not* use aluminum utensils.)

5. When juice starts to form on cabbage/salt mixture, pack tightly into crock using sanitized utensils or very clean hands. (I place a few whole leaves on bottom of crock, enough just to cover.)

6. Repeat until cabbage is 4 or 5 inches below top of container.

7. Pack down until cabbage is entirely submerged in the brine.

8. If there is not enough brine to cover cabbage, make more by mixing ½ tbsp kosher salt with 1 quart water; add cooled brine to crock until

all cabbage is completely covered. (I put a few whole leaves on top and submerge them as well.)

9. Once cabbage is submerged, fill a 2-gallon food-grade freezer bag with 2 quarts of water, seal, and place inside another 2-gallon bag; seal that.

10. Place this filled and twice-sealed bag on top of cabbage in crock, making sure it touches all edges and prevents air from reaching cabbage. (This is where the old-timers use a plate and stone.)

11. Cover crock tightly with plastic wrap, then cover with a cloth or towel. Tie tightly. Store the crock in a spot where the temperature is between 65 and 70 degrees Fahrenheit. (Note: I move the crock to a cooler room—say, 60 degrees—after 3 days.)

12. Fermentation will begin within a day and takes 3 to 5 weeks.

13. After 3 weeks, check for desired tartness. If you are going to can the sauerkraut, allow it to become more tart, as it will lose some of its tartness in the canning process.

14. Once fermented, sauerkraut can be eaten right away, frozen, or canned (follow canning instructions for your specific jars). I like it fresh.

OPEN-FACE
APPLE PIE

INGREDIENTS

7 Honeycrisp apples (or
apple of choice)

¾ cup sugar

2 tbsp butter

⅓ cup flour

¼ cup water

2 tbsp lemon juice

Cinnamon

9-inch pie crust

This apple pie just had to be part of this book, because nothing is more American than apple pie, and Brandywine Cottage is an American garden, complete with picket fence.

This recipe was passed along by Michael's mother, Eva Alderfer, and it is the one our families have made for years. It is simply more apple. In fact, the filling tastes almost like baked apples. Excellent warm or cold. It can be served plain, with vanilla ice cream, or with a piece of cheddar cheese.

METHOD

Preheat oven to 425 degrees Fahrenheit.

Peel and core the apples; slice and dice 2 and cut the remaining 5 into halves.

In a bowl, mix together sugar, butter, and flour to make crumbs.

Place one apple half in center of pie crust, cut side down, then arrange remaining apple halves in a circle around it. Fit the diced apple pieces among the halves, filling the pie. Sprinkle the crumbs evenly over the apples. Mix the water and lemon juice, and pour evenly over the apple filling. Sprinkle cinnamon on top.

Bake for 15 minutes at 425 degrees, then reduce heat to 375 degrees and bake for another 35 minutes, or until apples are tender.

opposite
Open-Face Apple Pie. Not only is it delicious, but I think it is like Brandywine Cottage—classical with a twist.

Epilogue

I LOVE SHARING MY GARDEN. I view it as a win/win situation. If people come and are inspired to create a garden, I win; if visitors think *I can do better!* and create a garden, I win again. Sharing comes naturally to most gardeners. It's how we learn. And the more gardens we plant, the more we help the planet.

I am just as concerned about the wider, wild garden, the *world* garden, as I am about my own garden here in Chester County, Pennsylvania. But I believe I can make the biggest difference, most rapidly, in my own garden. The axiom of "Think globally, garden locally" is true: each of us can inspire changes in the world via our own backyard.

I love the natural look and find inspiration in nature. As a gardener, I may not be able to duplicate nature, but I can try to catch her spirit. My overriding message has always been that ecology and aesthetics should meet in the garden. They are not mutually exclusive. Perhaps this speaks to our interpretation of what beauty is. Beauty is not perfection. I'm much more inclined to believe there is beauty in imperfection—or, as the traditional Japanese concept of *wabi-sabi* decrees, in beauty nothing is permanent, nothing is perfect. For me, beauty in the garden includes aging, and it includes creating habitats for other creatures, not just ourselves.

Every act of planting is an act of faith, of belief in tomorrow. In its small way, it is helping to ensure our future as a species. By planting just one tree and allowing it to mature, experts tell us, we contribute about 260 pounds of oxygen to the environment each year, or about a sixth of what each of us needs to survive. Biodiversity is essential, which is why we need to create or maintain habitats. Habitat destruction leads to loss of biodiversity in our ecosystems—as wildlife habitats shrink, species loss accelerates. But it has already been shown that if we create numerous small habitats—critter-friendly gardens, city parks, street trees—and link them together with green corridors, the loss of some species can be slowed or even reversed. Doesn't it feel good to be part of that process? People have played a large role in creating the problem; it's only fair that we become part of the solution.

Climate change is a reality. Our hope is that we are able to ameliorate its impact to some degree, one garden at a time. We can contribute to this by not planting lawns and other sterile monocultures, and by not using chemicals that kill off so many pieces of the life cycle. It's about learning to live with plants, and everything that comes with them.

When we create our gardens, we should try to choose plants not only for the way they look—although that is very important to me—but also to meet the needs of a variety of species that live in the garden and share this habitat with us. It's about the pollinator plants, for sure, but it's also about plants for the larvae to chew on as they grow; it's about planting trees and shrubs for the birds to nest in; leaving a few logs and sticks on the ground to house the beetles and bugs that the birds will eat. In many ways, our gardens help us to celebrate the connectivity of life. We are part of nature, too. It's man *with* nature—and unless we view it that way, we will lose.

This has been my life's message. You can make a garden. Everyone can. I'm not asking people to garden with the same intensity I do. But you can make a garden, and play a part in helping the earth heal. Every plant we grow is a vote for the future, whether it's in a single pot or a two-acre garden.

When I lecture, when I open my garden to visitors, in writing this book—the goal is always the same: how much richer your experience can be if you live with plants.

Your life and our planet will be better off as a result.

Resources

ANTIQUE ROSE
EMPORIUM
antiqueroseemporium.com

BRANDYWINE
SNOWDROPS
davidlculp.com/galanthus

BRENT AND BECKY'S
BULBS
brentandbeckysbulbs.com

BROKEN ARROW
brokenarrownursery.com

DIGGING DOG
diggingdog.com

EDELWEISS
edelweissperennials.com

FAR REACHES
farreachesfarm.com

GOSSLER
gosslerfarms.com

HIGH COUNTRY
highcountrygardens.com

JOY CREEK
joycreek.com

KEEPING IT GREEN
keepingitgreennursery.com

LOGEES
logees.com

OLD HOUSE GARDENS
oldhousegardens.com

PLANT DELIGHTS
plantdelights.com

RARE FIND
rarefindnursery.com

SWAN ISLAND DAHLIAS
dahlias.com

WOODLANDERS
woodlanders.net

Acknowledgments

I MUST CONFESS to being overwhelmed by the response to my first book about Brandywine Cottage, *The Layered Garden*. When we launched that book several years ago, I had no idea whether it would be successful—I was simply writing about something that I loved. But it seemed to take on a life of its own, and its success persuaded me to branch out into a series of lectures on that same theme. Thank you to all who bought the book and attended the lectures—you inspire me. And if I succeeded in getting someone to garden, I count myself successful. Now, with *A Year at Brandywine Cottage*, I hope to encourage you to embrace gardening—and nature—as a lifestyle, something that enhances every facet of life.

A very special thank-you to Michael Alderfer, who makes Brandywine Cottage a home as well as a garden. Without you, this would be a much different place. I am so pleased to be able to showcase your culinary skills in this book—and I thank your mother, Eva, for passing those skills along. A big thank-you also to family and friends who shared recipes with us. So many delicious dishes!

You are born with a family, and sometimes you are lucky enough to find another. The gardening community has been a large part of my "family" for much of my life. Rob Cardillo and Denise Cowie have, over the years, become a special part of that family. I consider them among the top in their respective professions of photography and writing. I admire their talents, but most of all, I thank them both for their kindness.

To Tom Fischer, Andrew Beckman, Franni Farrell, and the staff at Timber Press, a heartfelt thanks for your belief in me, and for all you do for American horticulture. To Bill Thomas and the entire staff at Chanticleer garden in Wayne, Pennsylvania, thank you for the use of your conference room to organize the photos and text for the book, and for the pleasure and inspiration Chanticleer brings to so many.

A big thank-you to everyone who has helped in the garden at Brandywine Cottage over the last few years: Kai Pedersen for your artful eye, stonework, watercolors, and plantsmanship; all the interns who've lent a hand during the past five years, including Josh Dunham, Lauren Kope, Brandon George, Timothy Hesslop, Spencer O'Bryan, Ted Banet, Tim Jerome, Aaron Wojtechi, and the entire "pantheon of garden gods" who helped hand-weed the meadowette in its second year; and Susie and Coleman Townsend, for your kindness and friendship, and for cheering me on and sharing with me the joys of garden-making.

Thank you also to Matthew Ross, plantsman and fellow horticultural cheerleader; and Queenie Northrop, my gardening pal, for reading the manuscript, for shared meals, and for the friendship you and Jack have shared with us through the years. And a posthumous thank-you to Joanna Reed, one of my gardening mentors, for introducing us, and for the countless gifts she gave to the gardening community.

There are so many others. The Galanthus Gala Committee, the Bondsville Mill Park Horticultural Committee . . . the list goes on and on. And so do my blessings.

Peace be with you.
David

Index

DAVID CULP is the creator of the gardens at Brandywine Cottage in Downingtown, Pennsylvania, which are listed in the Smithsonian Institution's Archives of American Gardens. He is the principle of David L. Culp Designs, owner of the galanthus nursery Brandywine Snowdrops, and the developer of the Brandywine hybrid strain of hellebores. He is also vice president of Sunny Border Nurseries in Connecticut. David has been lecturing about gardens nationwide for more than 25 years and is an instructor on herbaceous perennials at Longwood Gardens in Kennett Square, Pennsylvania.

David is the author of *The Layered Garden* (Timber Press), which won the 2013 Gold Medal from the Garden Writers Association for Best Overall Book. He is also a former contributing editor to *Horticulture* magazine. He serves on the Gold Medal Plant Selection Committee of the Pennsylvania Horticultural Society (PHS) and is a judge for that organization's prestigious Philadelphia Flower Show as well as the Northwest Flower & Garden Festival in Seattle. He also served as chairman of the Hardy Plant Society/Mid-Atlantic Group.

The gardens at Brandywine Cottage have been featured several times on the *Martha Stewart Living* television show and on HGTV, and articles about David have appeared in *Gardens Illustrated*, *Horticulture* magazine, and many other publications. He has received numerous awards, including the 2014 Garden Media Award from the Perennial Plant Association, a Distinguished Garden Award from the Pennsylvania Horticultural Society, and a PHS Award of Merit.

DENISE COWIE is a transplanted Australian journalist who worked as an editor, feature writer, and gardening columnist over the course of her 24 years on staff at the *Philadelphia Inquirer*. After leaving daily journalism, she added to her resumé by managing a website for a nonprofit consortium of public gardens, as well as writing and editing for magazines, books, and websites. She is an enthusiastic gardener who currently compiles the "Ask the Experts" column for *GROW* magazine. She has served on the boards of various nonprofit organizations, including Awbury Arboretum in Philadelphia. In 2006 she was named a Fellow of the Garden Writers Association of North America, and she has been a judge for that organization's national media awards.

ROB CARDILLO has been photographing gardens and plants, and the people who love them, for nearly 30 years. He's been credited as the primary photographer in over 25 books, including these Timber Press publications: *The Art of Gardening* (by R. William Thomas), *The Layered Garden* (by David Culp), and *Chasing Eden* (by Jack Staub and Renny Reynolds). Rob's work is also seen in such publications as *Country Gardens*, *Gardens Illustrated*, and the *New York Times*. Along with his Blue Root Media partners, Rob provides editorial content for an award-winning regional gardening magazine, *GROW*, published quarterly by the venerable Pennsylvania Horticultural Society. Winner of numerous photography awards, Rob was inducted into the Garden Writers Association Hall of Fame in 2015. You can see more of his work at robcardillo.com.

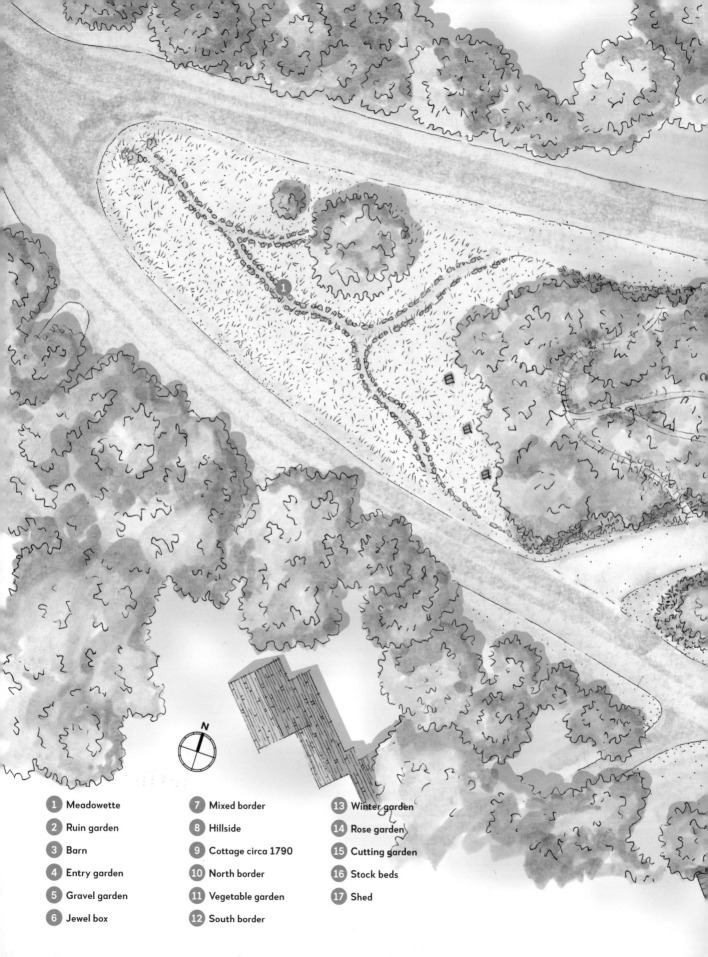

1   Meadowette

2   Ruin garden

3   Barn

4   Entry garden

5   Gravel garden

6   Jewel box

7   Mixed border

8   Hillside

9   Cottage circa 1790

10   North border

11   Vegetable garden

12   South border

13   Winter garden

14   Rose garden

15   Cutting garden

16   Stock beds

17   Shed